LOW
SUGAR

LOW
SUGAR

OVER 80 DELICIOUS RECIPES

Nutritionist Fiona Hunter
Project Editor Elizabeth Yeates
Senior Designer Vanessa Hamilton
Designer Saskia Janssen
Senior Jacket Creative
Mark Penfound
Pre-Production Producer
Rebecca Fallowfield
Producer Konrad Kirkham
Special Sales Creative
Project Manager Alison Donovan

First published in Great Britain in 2015 by
Dorling Kindersley Limited,
80 Strand, London WC2R 0RL

Material previously published in
The Diabetes Cooking Book (2010),
The Gluten-free Cookbook (2012),
Family Kitchen Cookbook (2013), and
Complete Family Nutrition (2014)

Copyright © 2010, 2012, 2013, 2014, 2015
Dorling Kindersley Limited
A Penguin Random House Company
001 – 284140 – Mar/15

A CIP catalogue record for this book
is available from the British Library.
ISBN 978-0-2412-0088-9

Printed in China

All images © Dorling Kindersley Limited
For further information see: www.dkimages.com

A WORLD OF IDEAS:
SEE ALL THERE IS TO KNOW

Contents

Introduction

The food we eat can have an important effect on our health and wellbeing. A healthy diet will help protect against diseases, increase resistance to colds and other infections, boost energy levels, help combat stress, and improve physical and mental performance. Eating well doesn't have to be difficult – you just need to know the key foods to include in your diet.

THE RECIPE FOR A HEALTHY DIET

The three key ingredients in a healthy diet are variety, balance, and moderation.

Variety

Your body needs over 40 different nutrients to accomplish every bodily task. No single food or food group – fruit and vegetables, proteins, carbohydrates, dairy, and fats – can provide all the essential nutrients, which is why you need to choose a variety of foods. The greater the variety of foods in your diet, the more chance you have of getting the key nutrients you need.

Balance

Ensure you eat the right amount of food from all of the food groups (see *Healthy eating in a nutshell*, right). Eating a balanced diet will provide your body with the energy and nutrients it needs. It will also keep your weight within its ideal range.

Moderation

Healthy eating doesn't mean giving up the foods you enjoy, it is simply a question of learning to eat them in moderation. By choosing natural and unprocessed foods and using cooking methods that use little or no fat (steaming and grilling for example), you can still enjoy all your favourite foods.

HEALTHY EATING IN A NUTSHELL

Eat a varied diet containing all of the food groups. Experts recommend the following guidelines:

• **Fruit, vegetables, and plant-based food:** eat plenty of fruit and vegetables and other plant-based foods, such as beans and pulses. You should have at least five portions a day, making up a third of your daily food intake.

• **Protein:** this includes meat, poultry, fish, and eggs. Aim to eat two to three small portions every day and always choose lean cuts of meat, with any excess fat removed.

• **Carbohydrates:** the body needs starchy (also known as complex) carbs to convert into energy. These include potatoes, cereals, and grains, plus bread and pasta. Eat at least five portions a day and choose wholegrains where possible.

• **Dairy:** milk, yogurt, and cheese provide us with essential calcium and other vitamins and minerals. Eat two to three low-fat portions a day.

• **Fats:** these should be eaten in moderation. Some fats are better than others: avoid saturated and trans fats, which are found in processed foods, as they clog arteries with cholesterol. Healthier unsaturated fats (poly- and monounsaturated) can reduce cholesterol levels, so it is always better to eat and use these. They are found in rapeseed oil and avocados.

HOW TO USE THE RECIPES

Icons These appear at the top of every recipe and advise on preparation and cooking times.

Cook's tip These give useful advice on how to adapt a recipe or how to prepare a certain ingredient.

Nutrition boxes The nutritional breakdown provides the amount of calories, protein, fat, carbohydrates, and sugar per serving.

The bitter truth about sugar

Eating too much sugar can increase the risk of tooth decay, high blood pressure, obesity, type 2 diabetes, and cardiovascular disease – but most of us are still consuming far too much of it! Low-sugar foods cooked at home are both tastier and healthier for your body than their processed counterparts.

A SPOONFUL OF SUGAR

Sugars can be divided into two groups: naturally occurring sugars, such as those found in fruit, and added or "free" sugars, which are often found in processed foods. The body treats both types of sugar in the same way; however, added sugars are considered to be less healthy – "empty calories" – because they provide energy without any accompanying nutrients. Foods with added sugar afford instant gratification, but this is soon followed by hunger and craving for something more.

Reducing your sugar intake can start with cutting down or omitting the sugar you add to coffee or tea, or sprinkle on cereal or porridge. Eat sugary foods such as biscuits, cakes, and puddings only in moderation, and try to eat naturally sugary foods, such as yogurt, or fresh or dried fruit, when you crave a sweet treat.

Cutting down on added sugar is only the start, as much of the sugar we consume is "hidden" in processed foods – foods that may not be considered as sweet. For example, one tablespoon of tomato ketchup contains around 4g (one teaspoon) of sugar. A simple and effective way to reduce the amount of sugar you eat is to cook as much as possible from scratch – that way you have ultimate control over how much sugar you consume.

READ THE SMALL PRINT

If you eat a lot of packaged foods, you're very much at the mercy of the manufacturers as to the amount of sugar you consume. Don't rely on the figures from the nutrition panel, as these include both naturally occurring sugars – such as fructose from fruit and lactose from milk – and added sugars. A pot of plain low-fat yogurt, for instance, may have 10g sugar, but that's natural sugar from the milk rather than added sugar. It's important not to consume any kind of sugar to excess, but try to go for foods containing naturally occurring sugar, as they provide the benefit of other nutrients, such as vitamins and minerals, along with a sweet taste.

If you want to know whether a product has added sugar, you need to look at the ingredients list rather than the nutrition panel. If a fruit yogurt contains added sugar (which most do), then sugar will appear in the ingredients list. By law ingredients must be included in descending order by weight, so the higher up sugar is on the ingredients list, the greater the quantity. It's also worth remembering that sugar is often disguised by using other names. If you see fruit juice concentrate, glucose syrup, molasses, corn syrup, dextrose, maltose, honey, brown rice syrup, grape juice, cane syrup, or evaporated cane juice, in the list of ingredients – that's code for sugar!

HOW LOW IS LOW?

For women, the current advice is to limit total sugar intake to no more than 90g a day. For men it is no more than 120g. While this may sound like a generous amount, it's very easy to exceed. Even if you don't add sugar to your tea, coffee or cereal in the morning, so many foods contain hidden sugar that you need to be careful. Some organisations recommend a more stringent reduction in our intake. In a recent report published by the World Health Organisation, it is suggested that we should try to reduce our intake of added sugars to no more than 5% of our total energy intake - which for an adult is around 25g (or 6 teaspoons) a day. The more sugar you eat, the more you want, so maintaining a low-sugar diet – rather than occasionally binge-eating sugary foods – is highly beneficial in the long term.

We do need some sugar for energy, but the processed ones added to our food are just not necessary. We can get all the sugar we need from fruit, vegetables, and grains, which are rich in vitamins and minerals.

Sweet tips
Instead of refined sugar and processed sweet snacks, try eating a small handful of chopped dried fruits mixed in with some chopped dark chocolate (70 per cent or more).

Make your own sweets by dipping slices of fruit (try banana, cherries, dried apricots, or figs) into melted, high-cocoa chocolate and allowing them to set on a sheet of baking parchment.

Some liquorice teas can fulfil the desire for something sweet, as can spiced or fruit teas.

BREAKFAST AND BRUNCH

Crumpets

Warm, toasted crumpets spread with a little butter
make a quintessentially British breakfast treat.

INGREDIENTS

225g (8oz) white bread flour
1 tbsp caster sugar
1 tsp fast-action dried yeast
½ tsp salt
250ml (9fl oz) milk
vegetable oil, for greasing
   and frying

SERVES 4      **PREP** 15 MINS,
PLUS RISING   **COOK** 20-25 MINS

1 Sift together the flour, sugar, yeast, and salt. In a pan, heat the milk with 250ml (9fl oz) water until lukewarm and stir into the flour. Beat well with a balloon whisk, then cover with lightly oiled cling film and leave to rise for 1 hour.

2 Heat a heavy frying pan and add a little oil. Lightly oil the crumpet rings and place them in the pan to heat up. Gently stir the batter and ladle enough into each ring to fill halfway. Cook over a low heat for 15–20 minutes; holes will appear on the surface of the batter and the batter will dry out.

3 Carefully remove the rings and turn the crumpets over to cook for a further 5–10 minutes on the other side. Transfer to a wire rack to cool and repeat until the batter is used up. Serve lightly toasted.

Nutrition data per serving

Energy	300kcals/1264kJ
Carbohydrate	48g
of which sugar	8g
Fat	8g
of which saturates	2g
Salt	0.6g
Fibre	2g

American-style pancakes

These light and fluffy pancakes are great for a weekend brunch.
Serve with crispy grilled bacon and maple syrup.

INGREDIENTS

125g (4¹/₂oz) plain flour
1 tsp baking powder
¹/₂ tsp salt
2 tbsp caster sugar
150ml (5fl oz) milk
2 eggs
15g (¹/₂oz) butter, melted
vegetable oil, for frying
grilled bacon and maple
 syrup, to serve

SERVES 5  **PREP** 10-15 MINS  **COOK** 15 MINS

1 Sift the flour, baking powder, and salt into a large bowl, and stir in the sugar. In a jug, beat together the milk and eggs, then add to the dry ingredients along with the butter. Beat the mixture until it's smooth and lump-free; it should have a soft, dropping consistency.

2 Heat a non-stick frying pan, add a few drops of oil, and swirl it around. Use a dessertspoon to carefully drop 2–3 rounds of batter in the hot pan; they should spread to about 9cm (3¹/₂in) in diameter. Reduce the heat to low.

3 After 2 minutes, flip the pancakes and cook the other side until golden brown and risen to 1cm (¹/₂in) thick.

4 Wrap the cooked pancakes in a clean tea towel to keep them warm while you cook the remaining pancakes. Serve each pancake with grilled bacon and maple syrup.

Nutrition data per serving

Energy	226kcals/944kJ
Carbohydrate	26g
of which sugar	8g
Fat	11g
of which saturates	3.6g
Salt	1g
Fibre	0g

American buttermilk "biscuits"

In America, "biscuits" (similar to British scones) are often served
at breakfast with bacon, sausage, or scrambled egg.

INGREDIENTS

300g (10oz) self-raising flour,
  sifted, plus extra for dusting
2 tsp baking powder
$\frac{1}{2}$ tsp fine salt
100g (3$\frac{1}{2}$oz) butter, chilled
  and cut into cubes
200ml (7fl oz) buttermilk
1 egg, lightly beaten

MAKES 6    **PREP** 10 MINS    **COOK** 10-12 MINS

1 Preheat the oven to 230°C (450°F/Gas 8). In a large bowl, or the bowl of a food processor, mix together the flour, baking powder, and salt. Add the butter and rub it in, or pulse-blend, until the mixture resembles fine breadcrumbs.

2 Make a well in the centre of the flour mixture and stir in the buttermilk. You will need to use your hands to bring the dough together. Gently knead the mixture on a floured work surface so that it forms a soft dough.

3 Gently roll the dough out to a thickness of 2.5cm (1in). Cut rounds out of the dough with a 7cm (2¾in) biscuit cutter. Gently bring the dough back together and re-roll it to cut out as many as possible.

4 Brush each biscuit with a little of the egg. Bake in the top of the oven for 10–12 minutes, until they have risen and are golden brown.

Cook's tip: The secret to light, fluffy biscuits is to handle the dough as little as possible, so cut them out close together to minimize the need to re-roll. Also, cut straight down with the biscuit cutter when you cut the biscuits out. If you twist the cutter as you work the dough, the edges of the biscuits will become compressed, stick together, and rise unevenly.

Nutrition data per serving

Energy	318kcals/1336kJ
Carbohydrate	37g
of which sugar	2g
Fat	16g
of which saturates	9g
Salt	1.5g
Fibre	2g

Breakfast burrito

A sort of total-breakfast-in-a-wrap, these American-inspired burritos are particularly popular with teenagers.

INGREDIENTS

12 smoked streaky bacon rashers

2 tbsp sunflower oil

250g (9oz) cooked, cold potatoes, cut into 1cm (½in) cubes

4 eggs

1 tbsp double cream

salt and freshly ground black pepper

6 tbsp tomato ketchup, plus extra, to serve (optional)

1 tsp smoked paprika

1 tbsp butter

4 x 20cm (8in) tortilla wraps

100g (3½oz) grated cheese, such as Cheddar

SERVES 4   **PREP** 20 MINS   **COOK** 10 MINS

1 Preheat the grill on its highest setting and grill the bacon until it is crispy. Meanwhile, heat half the oil in a large, non-stick frying pan, add the potatoes, and fry until crispy all over, then set aside. Wipe the pan with kitchen paper.

2 Whisk the eggs with the cream and season well. Mix the ketchup with the smoked paprika.

3 Once the bacon and potatoes are ready, make the scrambled eggs. Heat the butter in the frying pan and cook the egg mixture over a low heat until they are barely cooked and still quite loose. At the same time, lay out the tortillas and put 3 slices of bacon in a line across the middle of each. Top each with one-quarter of the potatoes, still keeping in a line across the centre, and add a smear of the spicy ketchup. Finish each by topping with one-quarter of the scrambled eggs and one-quarter of the cheese, again remembering to keep the filling in a compact rectangle down the middle of each tortilla.

4 To make the burritos, tuck the sides in over the filling, then roll the longer top and bottom edges up and over the filling, to make a parcel. Press down gently.

5 Heat the remaining oil in a clean frying pan. Put the burritos seam-side down into the pan and cook for 2–3 minutes over a medium heat, until golden brown and crispy. Press down with a spatula to seal the joins. Turn carefully and cook for a further 2–3 minutes. Depending on the size of your pan you may need to do this in 2 batches.

6 Serve the burritos sliced in half on the diagonal, with extra spicy ketchup (if desired).

Nutrition data per serving

Energy	724kcals/3023kJ
Carbohydrate	49g
of which sugar	7g
Fat	44g
of which saturates	17g
Salt	4.5g
Fibre	3.3g

Cheesy scrambled eggs on muffins

Turn simple scrambled eggs into an attractive brunch dish
with melting cheese, herbs, and toasted muffins.

INGREDIENTS

8 eggs

4 tbsp double cream

salt and freshly ground
black pepper

4 English muffins

50g (1¾oz) butter

100g (3½oz) finely grated
Red Leicester cheese

2 tbsp finely chopped
chives, plus extra to
serve (optional)

SERVES 4   **PREP** 5 MINS   **COOK** 5 MINS

1 Whisk the eggs and cream together, then season well. Slice the
muffins in half and set them to toast. Meanwhile, melt the butter
in a non-stick frying pan.

2 When the butter has melted, pour the egg mixture into the pan.
Cook gently for a minute or two, moving it about slowly with a
wooden spoon. Scatter the cheese and chives on top and continue to
cook until the eggs are soft and just set and the cheese has melted.

3 Pile the cheesy scrambled eggs on the toasted muffins and serve
with chives sprinkled over (if using).

Nutrition data per serving

Energy	599kcals/2499kJ
Carbohydrate	29g
of which sugar	2.6g
Fat	41g
of which saturates	21g
Salt	1.8g
Fibre	2g

Huevos rancheros

A classic Mexican dish of "ranch-style eggs" makes a substantial breakfast with a fabulous chilli kick.

INGREDIENTS

6 tbsp olive oil

1 onion, finely chopped

2 garlic cloves, crushed

2 dried chillies, finely chopped

1 scant tsp smoked paprika

400g can chopped tomatoes

½ tsp caster sugar

1 tbsp chopped flat-leaf parsley leaves

salt and freshly ground black pepper

300g (10oz) cooked waxy potatoes, cut into 2cm (¾in) cubes

200g (7oz) spicy chorizo, casing removed, cut into 2cm (¾in) cubes

4 eggs

2 tbsp chopped coriander leaves

SERVES 4    **PREP** 20 MINS   **COOK** 50 MINS

1 Heat 4 tablespoons of the oil in a small saucepan. Add the onion and fry over a medium heat for 5 minutes until softened. Add the garlic, chillies, and paprika, and fry for 1 minute. Add the tomatoes, sugar, and parsley, and bring to the boil. Season, reduce the heat, and simmer for 30 minutes. Set aside.

2 In a large, heavy-based frying pan, heat the remaining oil over a medium heat. Fry the potatoes for 5 minutes, add the chorizo, and fry for 5 minutes.

3 Take the pan from the heat and stir in the tomato salsa. Make 4 large holes in the mixture and crack the eggs into the holes. Return to the heat and fry for 5 minutes. Sprinkle with the coriander and serve from the pan.

Nutrition data per serving	
Energy	452kcals/1881kJ
Carbohydrate	21g
of which sugar	6g
Fat	32g
of which saturates	8g
Salt	1g
Fibre	3g

Eggs Benedict with smoked salmon

During pregnancy, recipes using raw or partially cooked eggs
should be avoided, or at least the eggs should be pasteurised.

INGREDIENTS

For the hollandaise sauce
100g (3¹/₂oz) unsalted butter
1 large egg yolk
¹/₂ tbsp lemon juice
salt and freshly ground
    black pepper

For the rest
4 eggs
2–4 English muffins
150g (5¹/₂oz) smoked salmon

SERVES 2    **PREP** 10 MINS    **COOK** 5 MINS

1 To make the sauce, melt the butter over a gentle heat, taking care it does not split. Put the egg yolk, lemon juice, and seasoning into a blender and whizz briefly. With the motor running, pour in the melted butter drop by drop, accelerating to a thin stream, until it has emulsified to a thick sauce. Serve it as soon as possible.

2 Meanwhile, boil a large pan of salted water, then reduce the heat to a low simmer. Crack an egg into a teacup and gently slide into the bubbling water. Repeat for all the eggs. Poach for 3 minutes, until the white is set, but the yolk is still runny. Remove with a slotted spoon.

3 At the same time, toast the muffins. If you like thick muffins use 4, cutting a thin slice off each one to add the egg, otherwise split 2 muffins horizontally to make 4 halves. When they are toasted, divide the salmon between them and top each with a poached egg and a little hollandaise sauce.

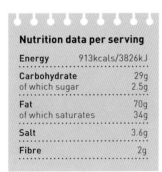

Nutrition data per serving	
Energy	913kcals/3826kJ
Carbohydrate	29g
of which sugar	2.5g
Fat	70g
of which saturates	34g
Salt	3.6g
Fibre	2g

Eggs Benedict with crispy bacon

Try this version of eggs Benedict with salty, crisp
bacon and crunchy walnut bread.

INGREDIENTS

For the hollandaise sauce
100g (3½oz) unsalted butter
1 large egg yolk
½ tbsp lemon juice
salt and freshly ground
black pepper

For the rest
6 smoked streaky bacon
rashers
4 eggs
4 thick slices of walnut bread,
or multigrain bread,
crusts removed

SERVES 2  **PREP** 10 MINS **COOK** 5 MINS

1 Make the hollandaise sauce as for Eggs Benedict with smoked
salmon (see opposite).

2 Meanwhile, preheat the grill on its highest setting. Cut each bacon
rasher in half horizontally, to make 12 short rashers, and grill the
rashers until crisp. Keep warm.

3 Next, poach the eggs. Boil a large pan of salted water, and reduce
the heat to a low simmer. Crack an egg into a teacup and gently
slide into the bubbling water. Repeat for all the eggs. Poach for
3 minutes, until the white is set, but the yolk is still runny. Remove
with a slotted spoon.

4 Meanwhile, toast the bread. Top each piece with 3 half rashers of
crispy bacon, a poached egg, and a little hollandaise sauce.

Nutrition data per serving	
Energy	934kcals/3913kJ
Carbohydrate	37g
of which sugar	2g
Fat	73g
of which saturates	36g
Salt	3.1g
Fibre	1.5g

Eggs Florentine

A great vegetarian option; make sure you drain the spinach before serving to prevent the toast going soggy.

INGREDIENTS

For the hollandaise sauce
200g (7oz) unsalted butter, plus
    1 tbsp extra for the spinach
2 large egg yolks
¾–1 tbsp lemon juice, to taste
salt and freshly ground
    black pepper

For the rest
250g (9oz) baby spinach leaves
4 eggs
4 thick slices of wholemeal
    bread, crusts removed

SERVES 2    **PREP** 15 MINS   **COOK** 5 MINS

1 Make the sauce as for Eggs Benedict with smoked salmon (see p20), adding lemon to taste.

2 Next, cook the spinach. Heat the extra tablespoon of butter in a large saucepan and add the spinach. Season it well and cook for a minute or two, stirring frequently, until it wilts completely. Drain well, squeezing out excess water, then return to the pan, mix in 2 tablespoons of the hollandaise sauce, and put the lid on to keep it warm.

3 Next, poach the eggs. Boil a large pan of salted water and reduce the heat to a low simmer. Crack an egg into a teacup and gently slide into the bubbling water. Repeat for all the eggs. Poach gently for 3 minutes, until the white is set, but the yolk still runny. Remove each egg with a slotted spoon.

4 Meanwhile, toast the slices of bread. When they are toasted, top each piece with a spoonful of creamy spinach, a poached egg, and a little hollandaise sauce.

Nutrition data per serving

Energy	1169kcals/4894kJ
Carbohydrate	31g
of which sugar	4g
Fat	104g
of which saturates	59g
Salt	1.6g
Fibre	5.3g

Salmon kedgeree

For an upmarket brunch, this delicious kedgeree with exotic saffron is just the ticket.

INGREDIENTS

300g (10oz) undyed smoked haddock fillets
300g (10oz) salmon fillets
200g (7oz) basmati rice
salt and freshly ground black pepper
pinch of saffron threads
60g (2oz) butter
4 hard-boiled eggs
2 tbsp chopped flat-leaf parsley leaves, plus extra to serve
lemon wedges and buttered wholemeal toast, to serve

SERVES 4  **PREP 20 MINS**   **COOK 20 MINS**

1 Place the fish in a single layer in a large frying pan. Pour over enough water to cover and heat gently to simmering point. Simmer for 5 minutes, then drain.

2 Meanwhile, cook the rice in boiling salted water with the saffron for 10–12 minutes, or according to the packet instructions. When it is cooked, drain, and stir in the butter.

3 Flake the fish into large chunks and add them to the rice, removing any tiny pin bones you find as you do so. Discard the skin.

4 Remove the yolks from the hard-boiled eggs and reserve. Chop the egg whites and stir into the rice. Add the parsley and season to taste with salt and pepper.

5 Divide the mixture between warmed plates and crumble the reserved egg yolks across the top with more chopped parsley. Serve with lemon wedges and triangles of buttered wholemeal toast.

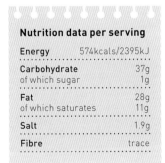

Nutrition data per serving

Energy	574kcals/2395kJ
Carbohydrate	37g
of which sugar	1g
Fat	28g
of which saturates	11g
Salt	1.9g
Fibre	trace

Savoury grits

An authentic Southern-style breakfast dish, made from ground
corn kernels, that is both hearty and filling.

INGREDIENTS

110g (3³/₄oz) instant grits
　(see Cook's tip)
125g (4¹/₂oz) mature Cheddar
　cheese, grated
50g (1³/₄oz) butter
1 tbsp sunflower oil
4 rashers smoked streaky bacon
freshly ground black pepper
splash of Tabasco sauce
　(optional)
handful of freshly grated
　Parmesan cheese
3–4 spring onions, finely sliced

SERVES 4　　　PREP 10 MINS　　COOK 10 MINS

1 Add 450ml (15fl oz) water to a large pan and bring to the boil. Tip in
the grits and stir, then cover and cook on a low heat for 5–8 minutes,
stirring occasionally, until they begin to thicken; or cook according to
the packet instructions.

2 Stir in the Cheddar and butter until melted, then simmer the mixture
for another 2–3 minutes until creamy. Remove from the heat.

3 While that is cooking, heat the oil in a non-stick frying pan, add the
bacon, and cook on a medium-high heat for 5–8 minutes until
crispy. Remove and transfer to kitchen paper.

4 Season the grits with lots of black pepper and add a dash of
Tabasco sauce, if you like. Spoon the mixture out into shallow
bowls or plates. To serve, crumble the bacon over the grits along with
the Parmesan and finally top with spring onions.

Cook's tip: Grits can be found in health food stores or online. If unavailable,
polenta is a good substitute: use the same weight of polenta mixed with the
same volume of water.

Nutrition data per serving

Energy	452kcals/1873kJ
Carbohydrate	19.5g
of which sugar	0.8g
Fat	33g
of which saturates	17g
Salt	1.7g
Fibre	1g

Potato farls

These Irish potato cakes can be fried or griddled – they are wonderfully creamy on the inside and crisp on the outside.

INGREDIENTS

675g (1½lb) floury potatoes, such as Maris Piper or Estima, skin on

salt and freshly ground black pepper

50g (1¾oz) butter

150g (5½oz) plain flour, plus extra for dusting

3 tbsp olive oil or a knob of butter, for cooking

crispy bacon and eggs, to serve

SERVES 4    **PREP** 15 MINS   **COOK** 40 MINS

1 Cook the potatoes in a large pan of boiling salted water for 20–25 minutes, or until tender when poked with a sharp knife. Drain and, when cool enough to handle, peel and mash. Add the butter and mash the potatoes until smooth.

2 Sift the flour into the mash, season well, and mix with a spoon. With your hands, bring the dough together. Turn it out onto a lightly floured surface and either roll or use the back of your hand to flatten it, so it is about 5mm (¼in) thick. Cut the dough out to make 4 x 6cm (1½ x 2½in) rectangles, then slice these into triangles.

3 To fry, heat a large, non-stick frying pan over a medium heat with half the oil or half the butter. Add half the potato cakes and fry for 2 minutes on each side, or until golden. Sit them on kitchen paper to drain. Repeat for the remaining farls and drain. To griddle, brush the griddle pan with a little oil, heat it to hot, add the farls a few at a time, and griddle for 2–3 minutes. Turn and cook the other side. Sit them on kitchen paper to drain. Repeat to cook the remaining farls. Serve for breakfast with crispy bacon and eggs.

Cook's tip: Cooking the potatoes with their skin on helps keep them dry. You can also use leftover mashed potato, but warm it slightly first. To reheat the farls from frozen, defrost overnight and reheat in a frying pan or microwave on a medium heat for 2 minutes, or in the oven at 180°C (350°F/Gas 4) for 10–15 minutes.

Nutrition data per serving

Energy	422kcals/1765kJ
Carbohydrate	55g
of which sugar	1.5g
Fat	19g
of which saturates	8g
Salt	0.2g
Fibre	4.5g

Potato, pancetta, and red onion hash

Cold, leftover boiled potatoes can be chopped up to turn
this hash into a quick brunch dish.

INGREDIENTS

salt and freshly ground
    black pepper
1kg (2¼lb) floury potatoes,
    such as King Edward or Maris
    Piper, peeled and cut into
    bite-sized chunks
1 tbsp olive oil
2 red onions, finely chopped
100g (3½oz) pancetta lardons
2 tbsp finely chopped chives
baked beans, to serve

SERVES 4    **PREP** 10 MINS   **COOK** 25 MINS

1 Bring a saucepan of salted water to the boil, add the potatoes, and
cook for 10 minutes. Drain.

2 Meanwhile, heat the oil in a large, non-stick frying pan over a
medium heat and cook the onions for 5 minutes. Add the pancetta,
season well, and cook for a further 5 minutes, stirring occasionally.

3 Add the cooked potatoes to the frying pan and cook over a high
heat for about 15 minutes, stirring frequently.

4 Divide the hash between warmed plates and sprinkle with the
chives. Serve with baked beans.

Nutrition data per serving	
Energy	300kcals/1263kJ
Carbohydrate	44g
of which sugar	4g
Fat	9g
of which saturates	2.5g
Salt	0.8g
Fibre	5g

Croque-madame

A once-in-a-while treat, this is the ultimate ham
and cheese toastie – try it and see.

INGREDIENTS

2 tbsp butter, plus extra for
   the bread
8 slices of good-quality
   white bread
200g (7oz) grated Gruyère
   cheese
1 tbsp Dijon mustard (optional)
salt and freshly ground
   black pepper
4 thick slices of good-quality
   ham, or 150g (5½oz)
   thinly sliced ham
1 tbsp sunflower oil
4 small eggs
shoestring fries, to serve

SERVES 4    **PREP** 10 MINS    **COOK** 10 MINS

1 Butter each slice of bread on both sides. Set aside 50g (1¾oz) of the
cheese. Make sandwiches by spreading 4 slices of bread with a little
mustard (if using), then a layer of grated cheese, firmly pressed down.
Season well, then add a piece of ham, another layer of cheese, and a
second piece of bread.

2 Melt the butter in a large, non-stick frying pan and fry 2 sandwiches
carefully over a medium heat for 2–3 minutes each side, pressing
them gently with a spatula, until golden brown. Keep warm while you
fry the remaining 2 sandwiches. Wipe the pan with kitchen paper.

3 Preheat the grill on its highest setting. Place the fried sandwiches
on a baking sheet and top each with one-quarter of the reserved
grated cheese. Grill until the cheese has melted and is bubbling.

4 Meanwhile, heat the sunflower oil in the frying pan and fry the
eggs how you like them. Top each sandwich with a fried egg and
serve with a pile of shoestring fries.

Nutrition data per serving

Energy	555kcals/2319kJ
Carbohydrate	31g
of which sugar	2.9g
Fat	34g
of which saturates	17g
Salt	3.3g
Fibre	1.8g

LUNCH

Beetroot and ginger soup

Earthy beetroot always makes a colourful soup. Here, ginger
adds a pleasant zing and the wasabi cream, swirled
in at the last minute, gives a fiery kick.

INGREDIENTS

500g (1lb 2oz) raw beetroot,
  stalks removed

salt

pinch of sugar

1 tbsp olive oil

bunch of spring onions, trimmed
  and finely chopped

5cm (2in) piece of fresh root
  ginger, peeled and grated

salt and freshly ground black
  pepper

750ml (1¼ pints) hot
  vegetable stock

3 tbsp soured cream

¼ tsp wasabi paste, or
  more if you like it hot

SERVES 4   **PREP** 10 MINS   **COOK** 55 MINS

1 To cook the beetroot, place them in a pan of salted water, add the
sugar, and bring to the boil. Cook on a low-medium heat, partially
covered with a lid, for 40 minutes, or until the beetroot is tender when
poked with a sharp knife. Drain and, when cool enough to handle, peel
and roughly chop the beetroot.

2 In a clean pan, heat the oil and add the spring onions. Cook for
2–3 minutes on a medium heat, just enough for them to soften,
then add the ginger and cook for a further minute. Add the chopped
beetroot and stir well to coat with the oil. Season, pour in the stock,
and bring to the boil.

3 Reduce to a simmer and cook gently for about 10 minutes, then ladle
into a food processor and blend until smooth, or use a stick blender.
Taste and season some more, if needed. Mix the soured cream with the
wasabi. Ladle the soup into bowls with a swirl of the wasabi cream.

Cook's tip: If you don't have wasabi paste, use hot horseradish sauce instead.

Nutrition data per serving

Energy	113kcals/475kJ
Carbohydrate	12g
of which sugar	12g
Fat	5.5g
of which saturates	2g
Salt	0.7g
Fibre	4g

Mexican sweetcorn soup with tortilla crisps

Make this easy-to-prepare soup as hot and spicy as you like,
and use plain crisps as an alternative topping.

INGREDIENTS

2 x 326g cans sweetcorn, drained
1 tbsp olive oil
50g (1³/₄oz) butter
1 onion, finely chopped
2 garlic cloves, finely chopped
¹/₂ tsp cumin seeds
3–4 red or green jalapeños in brine,
  drained and finely chopped
salt and freshly ground
  black pepper
pinch of cayenne pepper (optional)
leaves from a few sprigs of thyme
1 tbsp plain flour
1 litre (1³/₄ pints) hot vegetable stock
2 corn tortillas
handful of fresh coriander leaves,
  roughly chopped
lime wedges, to serve

SERVES 6  **PREP** 15 MINS   **COOK** 25 MINS

1 Pulse half the sweetcorn in a food processor until smooth. Heat the oil and butter in a large, heavy pan, add the onion, and cook over a low heat for 2–3 minutes until beginning to soften. Stir in the garlic, cumin, and jalapeños, cook for 1 minute, and season.

2 Add the cayenne and thyme and cook gently for 1 minute. Then remove from the heat, stir in the flour, and tip in the pulsed and whole sweetcorn. Pour in a little stock and return the pan to the heat. Bubble and stir, then add the remaining stock and bring to the boil. Reduce to a simmer and cook gently for about 15 minutes, or until the soup begins to thicken.

3 Preheat the grill to medium and lightly grill the tortillas for about 1 minute on each side, or until they start to crisp and bubble. Cut the tortillas into small triangles. Taste the soup and season again if necessary. Divide between bowls, top with the tortilla triangles and coriander, and serve with lime wedges.

Cook's tip: If you don't have a food processor, substitute a can of creamed sweetcorn instead of pulsing.

Nutrition data per serving

Energy	330kcals/1384kJ
Carbohydrate	32g
of which sugar	12g
Fat	11g
of which saturates	5g
Salt	1.4g
Fibre	2.5g

Quinoa vegetable soup

A light soup flavoured with orange, basil, and chilli – great when served with seeded brown rolls. Prepare the stock the night before for a more intense flavour.

INGREDIENTS

1 tbsp olive oil
1 onion, finely chopped
salt and freshly ground black pepper
1 garlic clove, finely chopped
½ tsp dried oregano
zest of 1 orange
3 carrots, diced
2 celery sticks, diced
150g (5½oz) broad beans, fresh
   or frozen, shelled weight
125g (4½oz) quinoa
handful of torn basil leaves
pinch of dried chilli flakes
grated Parmesan cheese and
   seeded brown rolls, to serve

For the stock

1 onion
2 cloves
1 carrot, cut into 4 pieces
1 celery stick, cut into 4 pieces
2 bay leaves
2 leeks, trimmed and
   roughly chopped
pinch of salt
1 tsp black peppercorns

SERVES 6  **PREP** 20 MINS  **COOK** 1 HR 30 MINS

1 For the stock, stud the onion with the cloves and place in a large pan with the carrot, celery, bay leaves, leeks, salt, and peppercorns. Add 1.4 litres (2½ pints) water and bring to the boil. Reduce to a simmer, partially cover with a lid, and cook for 1 hour on a low heat. Turn off the heat, cover, and leave for the flavours to infuse.

2 In a large, clean pan, heat the oil, add the onion, and cook for 5–6 minutes over a low heat until soft. Season, add the garlic, oregano, orange zest, carrots, and celery, and cook over a low heat for 10 minutes, or until the carrots soften. Stir in the broad beans and the quinoa. Strain the stock through a sieve into a large jug and discard the strained vegetables.

3 Add the stock, a ladleful at a time, to the pan with the softened vegetables and quinoa. Cook on a gentle simmer, adding enough stock until the desired consistency is reached. Bring to the boil and cook gently, uncovered, for 10 minutes, adding more stock if necessary, or until the quinoa is cooked. Stir through the basil and sprinkle with chilli flakes. Taste and season, if needed, and serve with grated Parmesan and seeded brown rolls.

Nutrition data per serving

Energy	140kcals/587kJ
Carbohydrate	21g
of which sugar	9g
Fat	4g
of which saturates	0.5g
Salt	0.28g
Fibre	6g

Smoked fish chowder

This soup is like a stew, full of nourishing fish, potatoes, and sweetcorn. Omit the bacon if you do not eat meat.

INGREDIENTS

½ tbsp olive oil

1 onion, finely chopped

1 leek, finely sliced

2 garlic cloves, finely chopped

4 unsmoked back bacon
   rashers, chopped

2 celery sticks, finely sliced

550g (1¼lb) floury potatoes, such
   as Maris Piper, cut into
   2.5cm (1in) cubes

700ml (1 pint 3½fl oz) fish stock

freshly ground black pepper

195g can sweetcorn (no
   added salt or sugar), drained

450g (1lb) undyed smoked
   haddock fillet, skinned and
   chopped into bite-sized pieces

2 tbsp chopped flat-leaf
   parsley leaves

wholemeal bread, to serve

SERVES 4-6   **PREP** 25 MINS   **COOK** 30 MINS

1 Heat the oil in a large pan over a medium heat. Fry the onion and leek for 5 minutes, until soft, but not browned. Add the garlic, bacon, and celery. Fry for 2 minutes.

2 Add the potato and stock, season well with pepper, and bring to the boil. Reduce the heat, cover, and simmer for 15 minutes, or until the potatoes are tender to the point of a knife.

3 Stir in the sweetcorn and haddock, cover, and cook for 3–5 minutes, or until the fish just starts to flake. Be careful not to over-cook the fish. Gently stir in the parsley.

4 Ladle the soup into pre-warmed bowls and serve with thickly sliced wholemeal bread.

Nutrition data per serving

Energy	348kcals/1472kJ
Carbohydrate	36g
of which sugar	8g
Fat	5g
of which saturates	1g
Salt	2.6g
Fibre	7g

French onion soup

Deep-flavoured and savoury, this recipe creates a soup
elegant enough to serve to friends.

INGREDIENTS

50g (1¾oz) butter

1 tbsp olive oil

1kg (2¼lb) white onions,
   finely sliced

2 garlic cloves, crushed

salt and freshly ground
   black pepper

2 heaped tbsp plain flour

150ml (5fl oz) white wine

2 litres (3½ pints) beef stock

a few sprigs of thyme

12 slices of baguette, each
   2cm (¾in) thick

150g (5½oz) grated
   Gruyère cheese

SERVES 6    **PREP** 10 MINS    **COOK** 1 HR 20 MINS

1 Heat the butter and oil in a large, heavy-based pan. Add the onions and cook over a medium-low heat for about 30 minutes, until dark golden brown and well softened. Add the garlic, season well, and stir in the flour for a minute or two.

2 Gradually stir in the wine and stock, add the thyme, and cook over a very low heat, uncovered, for 40 minutes, until the onions are meltingly tender and the soup reduced. Remove the thyme.

3 Preheat the grill on its highest setting. Grill the baguette slices on both sides. Divide the Gruyère cheese between the baguette slices, then melt it under the grill. Float 2 slices of cheesy toast on each warmed bowl of soup to serve.

Nutrition data per serving

Energy	502kcals/2103kJ
Carbohydrate	47.5g
of which sugar	11g
Fat	18g
of which saturates	10g
Salt	2.3g
Fibre	5g

Smoked mackerel salad

A packet of smoked mackerel is a great fridge standby, and
this healthy salad is a simple way of using it.

INGREDIENTS

salt and freshly ground
black pepper
550g (1¼lb) new potatoes,
well scrubbed and chopped
into bite-sized chunks
200g (7oz) hot-smoked mackerel
fillets, skinned
60g (2oz) baby salad leaves
2 tbsp chopped dill
2 tbsp chopped chives
200g (7oz) cooked beetroot (not
in vinegar), roughly chopped
baguette, to serve

For the dressing

4 tbsp extra virgin olive oil
juice of 1 lemon
1 tsp wholegrain mustard
1 tsp clear honey
1 garlic clove, finely chopped

SERVES 4  **PREP** 15 MINS **COOK** 10-15 MINS

1 Bring a large pan of salted water to the boil, add the potato chunks, and cook for 10–15 minutes, or until tender. Drain and set aside.

2 Meanwhile, break the mackerel into bite-sized pieces, removing any bones you find as you go, and place in a large serving bowl. Add the salad leaves and herbs, and gently toss together.

3 Place the dressing ingredients in a small jug, season, and whisk together with a fork.

4 Add the warm potatoes to the serving bowl, pour over the dressing, and stir gently. Add the beetroot and serve straight away with the baguette.

Nutrition data per serving

Energy	405kcals/1687kJ
Carbohydrate	27g
of which sugar	7.5g
Fat	27g
of which saturates	5g
Salt	1.2g
Fibre	3.5g

Chargrilled chicken Caesar salad

This has an easy version of the classic Caesar dressing, replacing
the traditional recipe made with raw egg.

INGREDIENTS

100g (3½oz) day-old baguette,
   or other rustic white bread
4 tbsp olive oil
salt and freshly ground
   black pepper
400g (14oz) skinless boneless
   chicken breasts
1 large Romaine lettuce, leaves
   broken into bite-sized pieces
30g (1oz) Parmesan cheese
   shavings

For the dressing
100ml (3½fl oz) extra virgin
   olive oil
1 tbsp Dijon mustard
3 tbsp good-quality mayonnaise
4 anchovy fillets, chopped
½ tsp Worcestershire sauce
1 garlic clove, crushed
2 tbsp finely grated
   Parmesan cheese
pinch of caster sugar

SERVES 4    PREP 20 MINS,
                                PLUS COOLING   COOK 20 MINS

1 Preheat the oven to 200°C (400°F/Gas 6). Trim the bread of any
crusts and cut into 2cm (¾in) cubes. Toss them with 3 tablespoons
of the olive oil, season well, and spread them out on a large baking
sheet, in a single layer if possible. Cook them at the top of the oven for
6–8 minutes, turning occasionally, until they are golden brown on all
sides. Watch carefully so that they do not burn. Set aside to cool. If you
do not have a chargrill pan, preheat the grill on its highest setting.

2 Meanwhile, rub the chicken breasts with the remaining olive oil,
season well, and either griddle in a chargrill pan or grill them under
the hot grill for 5 minutes on each side, or until cooked through and
nicely charred. Set aside to cool, then slice.

3 To make the dressing, put all the ingredients into the bowl of a mini
food processor, or into a suitable container for a hand-held blender,
and process or blend until they have emulsified into a thick, creamy
dressing. Season with pepper. To serve, put the lettuce in a large bowl
and toss it in the dressing. Scatter with the croutons and Parmesan
shavings and arrange the warm chicken slices on top.

Nutrition data per serving

Energy	593kcals/2467kJ
Carbohydrate	15g
of which sugar	2.5g
Fat	45g
of which saturates	9g
Salt	1.5g
Fibre	1.5g

Chorizo, chickpea, and mango salad

A hearty, main meal salad with great variety of flavour.

INGREDIENTS

1 tbsp olive oil

150g (5½oz) chorizo, roughly chopped

400g can of chickpeas, drained and rinsed

3 cloves of garlic, finely chopped

handful of flat-leaf parsley, finely chopped

1 tbsp dry sherry

2 ripe mangos, stoned, and flesh diced

small handful of fresh basil, roughly chopped

small handful of fresh mint leaves, roughly chopped

small handful of fresh coriander leaves, roughly chopped

250g (9oz) baby spinach leaves

SERVES 2   **PREP** 15 MINS   **COOK** 15 MINS

1 Heat the olive oil in a frying pan, add the chorizo and chickpeas and cook over a low heat for 1 minute, then add the garlic and parsley and cook for a further minute. Add the sherry and cook for 10 minutes, stirring occasionally.

2 Put the mango and remaining herbs in a bowl and toss together, then add the chickpea mixture and combine well. Spoon onto a bed of spinach to serve.

Cook's tip: Choose a full-flavoured, spicy chorizo, which will marry well with the chickpeas.

Nutrition data per serving

Energy	504kcals/2106kJ
Carbohydrate	31g
of which sugar	5.5g
Fat	24g
of which saturates	8g
Salt	1.5g
Fibre	2.5g

Egg salad

A step up from traditional egg mayonnaise, try this spread
on wholemeal toast for a quick, delicious lunch.

INGREDIENTS

6 eggs
6 tbsp good-quality mayonnaise
1 tbsp lemon juice
1 celery stick, finely chopped
1 heaped tbsp finely chopped dill
1 heaped tbsp Dijon mustard
1 large spring onion, finely chopped
salt and freshly ground
    black pepper
paprika (optional)

SERVES 4  **PREP** 10 MINS  **COOK** 10 MINS, PLUS COOLING

1 Bring a saucepan of water to the boil, lower in the eggs on a large spoon, and boil for 8 minutes. Remove with a slotted spoon, run under cold water, and leave to cool. Peel the eggs.

2 In a large bowl, beat together all the remaining ingredients, except the optional paprika, until well combined.

3 Finely chop the eggs and gently mix them into the mayonnaise mixture, being careful not to break up the eggs too much. Serve sprinkled with paprika (if using).

Cook's tip: Try using this as a filling for a delicious packed lunch, especially for children, as it is tasty, but not overpowering, and is also a good source of protein.

Nutrition data per serving

Energy	288kcals/1191kJ
Carbohydrate	0.5g
of which sugar	0.4g
Fat	27g
of which saturates	5g
Salt	0.6g
Fibre	0.2g

Grilled halloumi salad

Halloumi, traditionally a Cypriot sheep's cheese, is delicious served warm. Work quickly, as it hardens on cooling.

INGREDIENTS

250g (9oz) halloumi cheese with mint, cut into 8 slices

finely grated zest and juice of 1 lime

2 tbsp extra virgin olive oil

1 red chilli, deseeded and finely chopped (optional)

freshly ground black pepper

50g (1³/₄oz) pitted Kalamata olives

150g (5¹/₂oz) cherry tomatoes, halved

2 tbsp chopped coriander leaves

2 tbsp chopped flat-leaf parsley leaves

20g (³/₄oz) toasted pine nuts

70g (2¹/₄oz) rocket

4 pitta breads, warmed, to serve

SERVES 4    **PREP** 10 MINS, PLUS MARINATING    **COOK** 5-10 MINS

1 Place the sliced cheese in a single layer in a shallow dish. Evenly sprinkle over the lime zest and juice, oil, chilli, and a good grinding of pepper, and turn the cheese slices to coat them. Cover and set aside to marinate for 30 minutes at room temperature.

2 Meanwhile, place the remaining ingredients (except the pitta bread) in a large bowl and toss to combine. Divide the salad between 4 plates. Preheat the grill on its highest setting.

3 Line a baking tray with foil. Using a slotted spoon, remove the cheese from the marinade (reserve the marinade) and place on the tray. Grill for 3–5 minutes on each side, turning carefully, until golden brown. The cheese will not melt, but should soften slightly.

4 Place 2 slices of grilled halloumi on top of each plate of salad. Drizzle the reserved marinade evenly over each portion, to act as a dressing, and serve with warmed pitta bread.

Nutrition data per serving

Energy	305kcals/1270kJ
Carbohydrate	8g
of which sugar	1.5g
Fat	27g
of which saturates	12g
Salt	1.9g
Fibre	1g

Mixed bean and goat's cheese salad

The mealy beans complement the rich cheese.

INGREDIENTS

400g tin of butter beans, drained and rinsed

400g tin of flageolet beans, drained and rinsed

25g (scant 1oz) bunch of chives, finely chopped

2 tsp white wine vinegar

1 tbsp fruity olive oil, plus extra to serve

1 tbsp of fresh thyme leaves

pinch of chilli flakes

salt and freshly ground black pepper

50g packet of pea shoots

lemon juice, to season (optional)

100g (3½oz) semi-hard goat's cheese, broken up into pieces

SERVES 4  **PREP** 10 MINS

1 Put the beans in a large bowl and add the chives, vinegar, olive oil, thyme, and chilli flakes and stir to combine. Season well with salt and black pepper.

2 Stir through the pea shoots, taste, and add a squeeze of lemon if you wish. Transfer to a shallow serving dish and top with the goat's cheese, a drizzle of olive oil, and a twist of freshly ground black pepper. If you are a meat eater, you might try a little Serrano ham as an accompaniment.

Cook's tip: If you prefer, you could use a soft goat's cheese and toss it with the beans; it will become almost like a thick, creamy dressing. You can also substitute rocket for the pea shoots.

Nutrition data per serving

Energy	280kcals/1170kJ
Carbohydrate	30g
of which sugar	3g
Fat	11g
of which saturates	5g
Salt	0.2g
Fibre	8.5g

Double-decker turkey and avocado sandwiches

Serving layered sandwiches is an easy way to make
a simple sandwich more attractive.

INGREDIENTS

3 heaped tbsp good-quality
    mayonnaise
1 heaped tsp Dijon mustard
salt and freshly ground
    black pepper
butter, softened, for spreading
12 large slices of multigrain bread
2 handfuls of salad leaves
150g (5½oz) thinly sliced
    turkey breast
2 avocados, thinly sliced
juice of ½ lemon

SERVES 4    **PREP** 10 MINS

1 Mix the mayonnaise and mustard together and season well. Butter 8 slices of bread on one side only, and 4 slices carefully on both sides.

2 Lay 4 of the single side-buttered slices on a chopping board, buttered-sides up. Top each slice with one-quarter of the salad leaves, pressing them into the bread gently. Lay one-quarter of the turkey on top of each and spread over a thin layer of the mayonnaise.

3 Put a double-side-buttered slice of bread on each sandwich, then layer one-quarter of the avocado over each, drizzle with a little lemon juice, and season well.

4 Top each with a final slice of bread, buttered-side down, and press down well to hold everything together. Carefully trim the crusts off the bread and cut into halves on the diagonal to serve, or pack into a container for transportation.

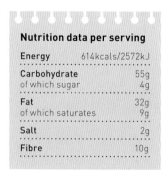

Nutrition data per serving	
Energy	614kcals/2572kJ
Carbohydrate	55g
of which sugar	4g
Fat	32g
of which saturates	9g
Salt	2g
Fibre	10g

Mexican eggs

This family favourite is a great way to turn eggs into a main meal. Add chilli if you want more heat.

INGREDIENTS

1 tbsp olive oil

2 garlic cloves, crushed

400ml (14fl oz) tomato passata

1 tsp smoked paprika

salt and freshly ground
   black pepper

1 tbsp chopped coriander
   leaves

4 eggs

4 thick slices of
   country-style bread

SERVES 4    **PREP** 5 MINS   **COOK** 25 MINS

1 Heat the oil in a 25cm (10in) heavy-based, ovenproof frying pan over a medium heat and fry the garlic for 1 minute until it begins to colour. Add the passata and smoked paprika and season well. Bring to the boil, reduce to a gentle simmer, and cook for 20 minutes until thickened and reduced.

2 Five minutes before it is ready, preheat the grill on its highest setting. Stir most of the coriander into the tomato mixture.

3 When the sauce is ready, take it off the heat. Make 4 holes in the sauce with the back of a spoon. Crack an egg into each hole and put the pan under the hot grill for 2–3 minutes, until the eggs have just set. Meanwhile, grill or toast the slices of bread.

4 Scoop a little of the tomato sauce over the top of each piece of toast, topped with an egg, and then sprinkle over the reserved coriander to serve.

Nutrition data per serving

Energy	228kcals/958kJ
Carbohydrate	22g
of which sugar	4g
Fat	10g
of which saturates	2.5g
Salt	1.2g
Fibre	2g

Chicken Caesar wraps

This delicious wrap, with its piquant dressing, has all the flavours
of a chicken Caesar salad in a portable form.

INGREDIENTS

1 tbsp olive oil

salt and freshly ground
  black pepper

2 skinless boneless chicken breasts

To serve

4 anchovy fillets

2 tsp lemon juice

2 tsp Dijon mustard

125g (4½oz) good-quality
  mayonnaise

4 heaped tbsp finely grated
  Parmesan cheese

½ tsp Worcestershire sauce

4 large wraps

4 large Romaine lettuce leaves

SERVES 4   **PREP** 10 MINS    **COOK** 15-20 MINS,
                                            PLUS COOLING

1 Preheat a griddle pan. Brush it with olive oil and season the chicken
breasts on both sides. Grill the chicken over a medium heat for
5–10 minutes on each side (depending on size), until charred in places
on the outside and cooked through. Leave to cool. If you are in a hurry,
slice it now into thin strips, as it will cool more quickly. Otherwise,
slice into thin strips once cooled.

2 While the chicken is cooling, make the Caesar sauce. Put the
anchovies and lemon juice in a bowl and mash them with the back
of a spoon until the anchovy has turned to paste. (Alternatively, use
a mortar and pestle.) Add the mustard, mayonnaise, Parmesan, and
Worcestershire sauce, and mix well. Check the seasoning and
add some pepper.

3 To assemble the wraps, lay them out on a work surface. Flatten the
lettuce leaves by pressing down on the central rib, and put a leaf onto
each wrap, with the leaf starting at the edge nearest you. Layer one-
quarter of the sliced chicken along the lettuce leaf, and top each line with
a good smear of the Caesar sauce, reserving a little to seal the wraps.

4 Take the remaining Caesar sauce and smear a little, with the back of
a spoon, all over each piece of wrap farthest away from you (it should
cover about one-third of the wrap). This will help stick the wrap together.
Then carefully roll up the wrap by picking up the side nearest to you and
folding it over the filling. Continue to roll it away from you until the
wrap bread meets itself and sticks together with the Caesar sauce.

5 Slice each end off carefully before cutting the wraps in half on a
diagonal to serve.

Nutrition data per serving

Energy	575kcals/2406kJ
Carbohydrate	40g
of which sugar	1.5g
Fat	33g
of which saturates	7g
Salt	1.7g
Fibre	2g

Roast beef, watercress, and horseradish mayo sandwiches

Sandwiches can be easily enlivened by flavouring some good, shop-bought mayonnaise

INGREDIENTS

3 heaped tbsp good-quality mayonnaise

1 heaped tsp horseradish sauce

salt and freshly ground black pepper

butter, softened, for spreading

8 large slices of sourdough or rye bread

2 handfuls of watercress

200g (7oz) rare roast beef, thinly sliced

SERVES 4 **PREP** 10 MINS

1 Mix the mayonnaise and horseradish together and season well. Butter each slice of bread on one side only.

2 Lay 4 of the buttered slices on a chopping board, buttered-sides up. Top each slice with a layer of the watercress, pressing it into the bread gently. Then layer one-quarter of the beef on each slice, and spread with a thin layer of the mayonnaise.

3 Top with the final slice of bread, buttered-side down, and press down well to hold everything together. Cut into halves to serve, or pack into a container for transportation.

Nutrition data per serving	
Energy	408kcals/1717kJ
Carbohydrate	37g
of which sugar	2.5g
Fat	18g
of which saturates	4g
Salt	1.4g
Fibre	2.5g

Roast beetroot, goat's cheese, and rocket sandwiches

These are fabulous for a picnic or packed lunch, or try them at home with toasted bread instead.

INGREDIENTS

4 small beetroot, approx. 75g (2½oz) each, peeled and sliced 5mm (¼in) thick

1 tbsp olive oil

salt and freshly ground black pepper

8 large slices sourdough or other rustic bread

butter, softened, for spreading

200g (7oz) soft goat's cheese

2 handfuls of rocket leaves

SERVES 4  **PREP** 10 MINS, PLUS COOLING  **COOK** 45 MINS

1 Preheat the oven to 200°C (400°F/Gas 6). Place the beetroot slices on a baking tray, brush them with the olive oil, and season them well. Bake them at the top of the oven for 20 minutes, turning once, until they are lightly browned and cooked through. Remove them from the oven and set aside to cool.

2 Spread the slices of bread with butter on one side only. Spread 4 slices with one-quarter each of the goat's cheese, season with a little pepper, then add a layer of the cooled beetroot slices.

3 Top the beetroot with a layer of the rocket and finish the sandwich with a final slice of bread, buttered-side down. Cut in half to serve, or pack into a container for transportation.

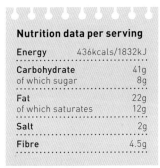

Nutrition data per serving	
Energy	436kcals/1832kJ
Carbohydrate	41g
of which sugar	8g
Fat	22g
of which saturates	12g
Salt	2g
Fibre	4.5g

Whole stuffed ciabatta with mozzarella and grilled vegetables

This is incredibly tasty and simple to transport,
and will easily feed a family of four.

INGREDIENTS

½ aubergine, cut into
    1cm (½in) slices
2 courgettes, cut into
    1cm (½in) slices
4–6 tbsp olive oil
salt and freshly ground
    black pepper
1 large beef tomato
1 ciabatta loaf
2 chargrilled red peppers
    from a jar, drained, and sliced
ball of mozzarella, approx.
    125g (4½oz), thinly sliced
handful of basil leaves

SERVES 4      **PREP** 10 MINS,
PLUS CHILLING   **COOK** 15 MINS,
PLUS COOLING

1 Preheat a large griddle pan or a grill on its highest setting. Brush the slices of aubergine and courgette on both sides with olive oil and season them well. Either griddle or grill them for 2–4 minutes each side, until they are charred in places and cooked through. Put them on a large plate in a single layer to cool.

2 Slice about 1cm (½in) off each end of the tomato, reserving these pieces. Slice the remaining tomato as thinly as possible.

3 Cut the ciabatta in half, leaving a hinge so you can open it out flat. Drizzle both sides with a little olive oil. Take the offcuts of tomato and rub both sides of the bread with the cut side, to soften and flavour the bread, then discard the offcuts.

4 Cover one side of the loaf with the aubergine, courgette, and red peppers, then top with mozzarella. Sprinkle with the basil, season, then add the tomato.

5 Close the loaf and press down on it hard. Wrap it very tightly in cling film, going round it a few times until it is completely covered and compressed. Leave in the fridge with a weight (such as a chopping board and some cans) on top for at least 4 hours, turning once. Unwrap and slice to serve, or transport in the wrapping and slice at a picnic.

Nutrition data per serving

Energy	435kcals/1812kJ
Carbohydrate	36g
of which sugar	4g
Fat	25g
of which saturates	6.5g
Salt	1.2g
Fibre	8g

Mozzarella en carrozza

These Italian-style fried sandwiches are rich, crispy,
and oozing with melted mozzarella.

INGREDIENTS

2 balls of mozzarella cheese,
approx. 125g (4½oz) each, sliced

8 thick slices of white bread,
crusts removed

4 tbsp plain flour

salt and freshly ground
black pepper

2 eggs

2 tbsp milk

2 tbsp olive oil

SERVES 4    **PREP** 15 MINS    **COOK** 10-15 MINS

1 Carefully pat each of the mozzarella slices dry with kitchen paper; be gentle and try not to tear them. Arrange them evenly over 4 slices of the bread, leaving a 1cm (½in) gap all round the edges to act as a border.

2 Place the remaining slices of bread on top of the cheese and press the bread together all round the edges.

3 Put the flour on a plate and season well. Beat the eggs and milk in a shallow dish, large enough for a sandwich to fit in, and whisk together with a fork until well combined.

4 Heat half the oil in a large, non-stick frying pan over a medium heat. Coat one of the sandwiches in the flour and then in the egg mixture. Add to the pan. Repeat with the second sandwich. Cook for 2–3 minutes on each side, turning once, until golden brown. Take care that they do not scorch; reduce the heat slightly if they threaten to do so. Remove and keep warm.

5 Add the remaining oil to the pan and cook the last 2 sandwiches. Serve immediately.

Nutrition data per serving

Energy	500kcals/2092kJ
Carbohydrate	48g
of which sugar	2.5g
Fat	23g
of which saturates	11g
Salt	1.8g
Fibre	2.2g

Summer pasta salad

Kids love pasta, so try to expand their horizons with this tasty Italian-style pasta salad.

INGREDIENTS

salt and freshly ground
  black pepper
250g (9oz) dried pasta,
  such as farfalle
150g (5½oz) cherry tomatoes
150g (5½oz) bocconcini (mini
  mozzarella cheese balls), drained
2 avocados, cut into large chunks
60g (2oz) pitted black olives
large handful of basil leaves
juice of 1 lemon
75ml (2½fl oz) extra virgin olive oil
1 tsp Dijon mustard
2 tbsp chopped chives
1 garlic clove, finely chopped

SERVES 4    **PREP** 20 MINS    **COOK** 10-12 MINS

1 Bring a large pan of salted water to the boil and cook the pasta according to the packet instructions. Drain and rinse under cold running water until the pasta is cold. Drain well and set aside.

2 Place the tomatoes, bocconcini, avocados, and olives in a large serving bowl. Tear the basil leaves and add to the bowl. Season well and toss carefully to combine.

3 In a jug, combine the lemon juice, oil, mustard, chives, and garlic. Season and stir well.

4 Add the cold pasta to the bowl and pour over the dressing. Stir gently but well and serve with warm ciabatta.

Cook's tip: If you find it hard to get hold of bocconcini, buy a ball of fresh mozzarella and dice it into pieces a little smaller than the cherry tomatoes.

Nutrition data per serving	
Energy	611kcals/2554kJ
Carbohydrate	47g
of which sugar	3g
Fat	40g
of which saturates	10g
Salt	0.6g
Fibre	7g

Pancetta and pea frittata

A frittata is basically a grilled omelette, and a mainstay of Italian family cooking. This one makes a great lunch.

INGREDIENTS

1 tbsp olive oil

100g (3½oz) pancetta lardons

6 eggs

1 tbsp double cream

25g (scant 1oz) finely grated Parmesan cheese

salt and freshly ground black pepper

100g (3½oz) frozen peas

1 tbsp butter

SERVES 4-6    **PREP** 10 MINS    **COOK** 15 MINS, PLUS RESTING

1 Heat the oil in a 25cm (10in) heavy-based, ovenproof frying pan. Fry the pancetta for 3–5 minutes until it starts to brown at the edges. Set aside. Wipe the pan with kitchen paper. Preheat the grill on its highest setting.

2 Whisk together the eggs, cream, and Parmesan, and season well (go easy on the salt, as the Parmesan and pancetta are salty). Add the peas (they will cook in the frittata) and pancetta, and mix well.

3 Melt the butter in the frying pan over a medium heat and pour in the egg mixture. Cook for 5 minutes, without moving the mixture, until the edges start to set.

4 Transfer the pan to the grill and cook for 5 minutes until the frittata is set and golden brown. Rest for at least 5 minutes. Cut into wedges and serve warm or at room temperature.

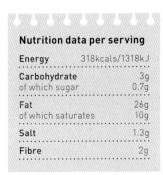

Nutrition data per serving

Energy	318kcals/1318kJ
Carbohydrate	3g
of which sugar	0.7g
Fat	26g
of which saturates	10g
Salt	1.3g
Fibre	2g

Auvergne torte

This warming pie from France is an ideal lunch when it's cold outside; it's very comforting in the depths of winter.

INGREDIENTS

For the filling

30g (1oz) butter

1 large onion, finely sliced

1 garlic clove, finely chopped

100g (3½oz) bacon lardons

650g (1lb 6oz) waxy new potatoes, peeled and finely sliced

100g (3½oz) Cantal cheese, or Wensleydale or mild Cheddar, grated

1 tbsp finely chopped flat-leaf parsley

salt and freshly ground black pepper

200ml (7fl oz) single cream

1 egg yolk

For the pastry

500g (1lb 2oz) ready-made puff pastry

plain flour, for dusting

1 egg yolk, beaten with 1 tbsp cold water, to glaze

SERVES 8   **PREP** 30 MINS, PLUS CHILLING   **COOK** 1 HR 15 MINS

1 Melt the butter in a large saucepan. Add the onion and cook over a medium heat for 10 minutes. Add the garlic and bacon and cook for a further 5 minutes until the onion is soft, but not brown.

2 Preheat the oven to 180°C (350°F/Gas 4). Roll out the puff pastry on a floured surface and, using a 23cm (9in) deep-dish metal pie tin as a template, cut from one end a circle large enough to top the pie. Use the rest of the pastry to line the tin, leaving a 1cm (½in) overhang around the edges. Wrap and chill the base and the top for 20 minutes.

3 Brush the inside of the pastry case, including the edges, with some of the egg yolk mixture. Reserve the remainder.

4 Layer the pastry case with one-third of the potatoes. Cover them with half the onion and bacon mixture and half the cheese. Scatter over half the parsley and season with salt and pepper.

5 Repeat the procedure and finish with a final layer of potatoes. Whisk together the cream and the egg yolk, and pour it over the pie filling. Top the pie with the pre-cut circle of pastry, pressing it down around the edges to seal. Crimp the edges.

6 Brush the top of the pie with the remaining egg yolk mixture and cut 2 small slits in the top to allow steam to escape. Place the pie on a baking tray and bake for 1 hour until well cooked, puffed up, and golden brown. Set aside to rest for 15–20 minutes before serving.

Nutrition data per serving	
Energy	476kcals/1990kJ
Carbohydrate	37g
of which sugar	3g
Fat	31g
of which saturates	16g
Salt	1.3g
Fibre	3g

Fish tacos

Anything served in a wrap is a sure family favourite, as it enables everyone to assemble their own wrap as they like.

INGREDIENTS

400g (14oz) firm-fleshed white
  fish, cut into 2cm (¾in) cubes
4 tbsp plain flour
2 eggs, lightly beaten
125g (4½oz) fine polenta
1 tsp smoked paprika
salt and freshly ground black
  pepper
sunflower oil, for frying

To serve

8 tortillas or wraps, warmed
lettuce leaves or green salad
finely sliced red onion
  or spring onions
tomato salsa
guacamole
Greek yogurt or soured cream
hot sauce
lime wedges

SERVES 4    **PREP** 5 MINS,
PLUS RESTING    **COOK** 10 MINS

1 Pat the fish dry with kitchen paper. Lay the flour, eggs, and polenta out in 3 wide, shallow bowls. Toss the flour with the smoked paprika and season it well.

2 Coat the fish pieces by dusting them first with the seasoned flour, then dipping them in the eggs, then rolling in the polenta, until they are well covered. Put them on a plate, cover with cling film, and rest in the fridge for 30 minutes. This helps the coating to stick.

3 Heat a 1cm (½in) depth of oil in a large, deep-sided frying pan. Fry the fish chunks for 2 minutes on each side, turning them carefully, until golden brown and crispy all over. Do not crowd the pan; you may need to cook in 2 batches. Rest on a plate lined with kitchen paper while you cook the rest.

4 Serve the fish with the warmed tortillas and the selection of accompaniments for everyone to assemble their own wraps.

Nutrition data per serving

Energy	656kcals/2769kJ
Carbohydrate	99g
of which sugar	1.5g
Fat	12g
of which saturates	2g
Salt	1.2g
Fibre	5.5g

Spiced lemony lentils with roast potatoes

A tasty vegetarian dish, made more substantial by the inclusion of chickpeas and roast potatoes.

INGREDIENTS

175g (6oz) Puy lentils, rinsed and any grit removed

900ml (1½ pints) vegetable stock

salt and freshly ground black pepper

3 potatoes, peeled and cut into 2.5cm (1in) cubes

2 tbsp olive oil

2 red chillies, deseeded and finely chopped

2 tsp cumin seeds

2 garlic cloves, finely chopped

zest of 1 lemon

1 onion, finely chopped

1 red pepper, deseeded and finely chopped

400g can chickpeas, drained and rinsed

juice of 2 lemons

1 tbsp flat-leaf parsley, finely chopped

SERVES 4   **PREP** 15 MINS    **COOK** 40-50 MINS

1 Preheat the oven to 200°C (400°F/Gas 6). Put the lentils in a large pan and cover with the stock. Season well and bring to the boil, remove any scum on the surface of the liquid, and then simmer gently for 30–40 minutes, or until the lentils are soft. (If the lentils look as if they are drying out, top up with a little more stock.) Drain and set aside.

2 While the lentils are cooking, toss the potatoes in 1 tablespoon of the olive oil and put them in a large roasting tin along with the chillies and cumin seeds. Season well with salt and black pepper. Roast in the oven for 30–35 minutes, giving them a shake or a stir halfway through, and add the garlic and lemon zest at the same time.

3 Heat the remaining oil in a large, heavy, deep frying pan. Add the onion and red pepper, and cook for about 5 minutes or until the pepper softens. Tip in the chickpeas and the cooked lentils, stir well, and then stir in the lemon juice and parsley. If you prefer a wetter mixture, add a little hot stock and let it cook for a few minutes. Serve topped with a spoonful of the crispy roast potatoes.

Nutrition data per serving

Energy	456kcals/1925kJ
Carbohydrate	67g
of which sugar	7g
Fat	9g
of which saturates	1.5g
Salt	1.1g
Fibre	7g

DINNER

Salmon in foil

Baking in foil keeps the flavours in the fish and the smells out
of the kitchen, and saves on the washing up, too!

INGREDIENTS

1 tbsp olive oil

4 salmon fillets, approx.
100g (3½oz) each

salt and freshly ground
black pepper

2 lemons

50g (1¾oz) butter, cut
into cubes

bunch of chives

new potatoes and steamed
green vegetables, to serve

SERVES 4 **PREP** 10 MINS  **COOK** 20-25 MINS

1 Preheat the oven to 180°C (350°F/Gas 4). Line a shallow ovenproof dish, large enough to hold all the salmon fillets, with a piece of foil that will be big enough to wrap over the top of the fillets completely. Brush the foil with the oil.

2 Place the salmon on the foil, skin-side down, and season well. Squeeze the juice from one lemon and drizzle it over the fish. Slice the second lemon into quarters and place a slice centrally on each fillet, to release juice and baste the fish as it bakes.

3 Arrange the butter over and around the salmon and place the whole chives over the fish. Bring the edges of the foil together to make a sealed parcel.

4 Bake in the oven for 20–25 minutes, depending on the size of the fillets. Remove the lemon slices and chives from the foil and discard.

5 Transfer the fish to warmed serving plates. Drizzle the lemon butter from the foil over the salmon and serve with new potatoes and steamed green vegetables.

Nutrition data per serving

Energy	300kcals/1234kJ
Carbohydrate	0g
of which sugar	0g
Fat	24g
of which saturates	9g
Salt	0.3g
Fibre	0g

Salmon and potato gratin

This rich, creamy dish would convert anyone to the joys
of eating oily fish. It's immensely comforting, too.

INGREDIENTS

800g (1¾lb) potatoes,
 peeled weight
salt and freshly ground
 black pepper
butter, softened, for greasing
2 heaped tbsp finely chopped dill
350g (12oz) skinless salmon fillets,
 cut into 2cm (¾in) chunks
200ml (7fl oz) single cream
150ml (5fl oz) fish stock or
 vegetable stock

SERVES 4   **PREP 15 MINS**   **COOK 1 HR**

1 Preheat the oven to 190°C (375°F/Gas 5). Cut the potatoes into
5mm- (¼in-) thick slices. Bring them to the boil in a large pan of
salted water and simmer for 5 minutes, until part-cooked. Drain well.
Rub a 25cm- (10in-) ovenproof dish with the butter.

2 Layer half the potato slices in the dish. Sprinkle the dill on the
potatoes, lay the salmon over in a single layer, and season well. Top
with the rest of the potatoes, making sure that the final layer looks neat.

3 Whisk the cream and stock together, pour it over the potatoes, and
cook for 50 minutes to 1 hour, until the top is crispy and the
potatoes cooked through.

Cook's tip: Salmon can be expensive, but should be part of a family's diet as it is
rich in healthy omega–3 fatty acids. Try buying the more inexpensive tail fillets,
which are perfect for this dish.

Nutrition data per serving

Energy	423kcals/1769kJ
Carbohydrate	33g
of which sugar	2g
Fat	22g
of which saturates	9g
Salt	0.6g
Fibre	3.5g

Grilled salmon and salsa verde

A simple, tasty meal that takes just minutes to prepare,
but tastes piquant and sophisticated.

INGREDIENTS

4 salmon fillets, approx.
   150g (5½oz) each
150ml (5fl oz) extra virgin olive oil,
   plus extra for rubbing
salt and freshly ground
   black pepper
15g (½oz) basil leaves
15g (½oz) flat-leaf parsley leaves
15g (½oz) mint leaves
3 tbsp lemon juice
6 anchovy fillets
1 tbsp capers, rinsed
2 tsp Dijon mustard
1 garlic clove, crushed
mashed potato, to serve
4 lemon wedges, to serve

SERVES 4  **PREP** 5 MINS **COOK** 5 MINS

1 Preheat the grill on its highest setting. Rub the salmon with a little oil and season it well on both sides. Grill it for 3–5 minutes on each side (depending on its thickness), until crispy outside and moist within.

2 Meanwhile, to make the salsa verde, put all the remaining ingredients except the oil into the bowl of a small food processor. Whizz to a rough paste, then pour in the oil in a thin stream, still processing, until you have a thick, vibrant, green sauce (you may not need all the oil). Season to taste.

3 Serve the fish on mashed potato with the salsa verde poured over the top and a lemon wedge on the side.

Nutrition data per serving	
Energy	541kcals/2242kJ
Carbohydrate	0.5g
of which sugar	0.5g
Fat	46g
of which saturates	7g
Salt	1g
Fibre	0g

Asian-style crispy fish

A medley of vegetables topped with pan-fried red mullet
and seasoned with a Vietnamese-style dressing.

INGREDIENTS

4 red mullet, gurnard or sea
   bass fillets, skinned

1 tbsp rice flour

1 tbsp sunflower oil

**For the noodles and
   vegetables**

250g (9oz) vermicelli rice noodles

200g (7oz) pak choi, trimmed
   and shredded

2 carrots, grated

handful of beansprouts

4 spring onions, finely sliced

handful of mint leaves, torn

handful of Thai basil leaves or
   regular basil, torn

handful of fresh coriander leaves

1 tbsp sesame seeds, to garnish

For the dressing

juice of 2 limes

2 tbsp rice wine vinegar

nam pla (fish sauce), to taste

SERVES 4    **PREP** 20 MINS   **COOK** 15 MINS

1 For the dressing, mix together the lime juice and rice wine vinegar.
Add the nam pla to taste, and set aside.

2 Toss the fish fillets in the rice flour, heat the oil in the wok or pan,
and add them to the hot oil. Cook 2 at a time on a medium-high
heat for about 4–6 minutes, turning halfway until golden and crispy.
Remove with a fish slice and set aside on a plate layered with kitchen
paper, to drain. Repeat to cook the remaining fillets.

3 Sit the noodles in a bowl, pour over boiling water to cover, and
leave for 3–4 minutes, according to the packet instructions. Drain
well, separate the strands if needed, and set aside to cool. In a large
bowl, place the shredded pak choi, grated carrot, and half the dressing
and toss. Add the beansprouts, spring onions, and cooled noodles and
toss again with the remaining dressing. Add half the herbs, toss, and
transfer to a serving dish. Top with the fish fillets and sprinkle over
the remaining herbs and sesame seeds.

Nutrition data per serving

Energy	488kcals/2043kJ
Carbohydrate	56g
of which sugar	5g
Fat	11g
of which saturates	1g
Salt	0.6g
Fibre	4g

Fish pie

Try to use small, cold-water prawns in this dish, which are
tastier and also less likely to have been farmed.

INGREDIENTS

300g (10oz) skinless salmon fillet

200g (7oz) skinless smoked
 haddock fillet

50g (1¾oz) unsalted butter

5 tbsp plain flour, plus extra
 for dusting

350ml (12fl oz) whole milk

salt and freshly ground
 black pepper

pinch of grated nutmeg

200g (7oz) cooked prawns,
 shelled and deveined

100g (3½oz) baby spinach

250g (9oz) shop-bought puff
 pastry, preferably all-butter

1 egg, lightly beaten, for glazing

SERVES 4   PREP 20 MINS,
              PLUS RESTING    COOK 30-35 MINS

1 Preheat the oven to 200°C (400°F/Gas 6). Poach the salmon and
 haddock in simmering water for 5 minutes. Drain and cool.

2 Melt the butter in a pan. Remove from the heat and whisk in the
 flour until a paste is formed. Gradually add the milk, whisking
to avoid any lumps. Season well and add the nutmeg. Bring the sauce
to the boil, reduce the heat, and cook for 5 minutes, stirring.

3 Flake the fish into a bowl and add the prawns. Spread the uncooked
 spinach over the top and pour the hot sauce over it. Season to taste.
When the spinach has wilted, mix the filling together and transfer to
an 18cm (7in) pie dish.

4 On a floured surface, roll out the pastry to a shape bigger than
 the pie dish, 3–5mm (⅛–¼in) thick. Cut a shape to fit the pie.
Roll some of the trimmings out into long strips. Brush the rim of the
dish with some egg and press the pastry strips around the rim.

5 Brush the edging with egg and top with the pastry lid. Press down
 to seal the lid, and trim off any overhang. Brush the top with egg
and cut 2 slits in it. Bake in the top of the oven for 20–25 minutes until
golden, and allow to rest for 5 minutes before serving.

Nutrition data per serving	
Energy	694kcals/2908kJ
Carbohydrate	40g
of which sugar	5g
Fat	39g
of which saturates	17g
Salt	2.5g
Fibre	2.8g

Spanish fish stew

Give everyday white fish a piquant, hearty Spanish twist with
chorizo and olives to liven up a midweek meal.

INGREDIENTS

280g jar roasted peppers in
oil, drained and chopped
(oil reserved)

2 red onions, cut into chunks

1 garlic clove, finely chopped

175ml (6fl oz) dry white wine

500g (1lb 2oz) new potatoes,
scrubbed, unpeeled, and
chopped into large chunks

175g (6oz) chorizo,
roughly chopped

500g jar passata

salt and freshly ground
black pepper

450g (1lb) white fish fillets, such
as pollock, skinned and cut
into chunks

40g (1¼oz) pitted green olives

crusty bread, to serve

SERVES 4    **PREP** 15 MINS   **COOK** 1 HR 30 MINS

1 Preheat the oven to 160°C (325°F/Gas 3). Heat 1 tablespoon of oil from the roasted pepper jar in a large, heavy-based flameproof casserole over a medium heat.

2 Fry the onions for 10 minutes, until softened, but not browned, then add the garlic for 1 minute.

3 Pour in the wine, increase the heat, and allow to bubble away until the liquid is reduced to about one-half of its original volume. Stir occasionally to prevent the onions from catching on the casserole.

4 Add the potatoes, chorizo, passata, and chopped peppers. Stir in 1 further tablespoon of the reserved oil from the peppers and season well. Bring to the boil, cover, and cook in the oven for 1 hour.

5 Remove from the oven and stir the fish and olives into the casserole. Return to the oven for a further 15 minutes. Serve in warmed bowls with crusty bread.

Nutrition data per serving

Energy	443kcals/1860kJ
Carbohydrate	33g
of which sugar	5.5g
Fat	16.5g
of which saturates	4g
Salt	0.9g
Fibre	7g

Moules marinière

Discard any mussels that do not close firmly
when sharply tapped on the sink.

INGREDIENTS

1 tbsp olive oil
30g (1oz) butter
1 onion, roughly chopped
2 celery sticks, finely chopped
1 carrot, finely chopped
2 garlic cloves, finely chopped
120ml (4fl oz) dry white wine
1.5kg (3lb 3oz) live mussels,
    scrubbed and beards removed
freshly ground black pepper
120ml (4fl oz) double cream
leaves from 1 bunch of flat-leaf
    parsley, finely chopped
baguette, to serve

SERVES 4   **PREP** 25 MINS   **COOK** 10 MINS

1 Heat the oil and butter in a large pan, big enough easily to hold all the mussels, over a medium heat, and gently fry the onion, celery, carrot, and garlic for 5 minutes, stirring occasionally.

2 Add the wine and mussels and season with pepper. Increase the heat and bring to the boil. Cover and cook for 5 minutes, shaking the pan occasionally. Discard any mussels that do not open, and warn your guests to do the same.

3 Stir in the cream and parsley. Serve the mussels straight away with chunks of baguette.

Nutrition data per serving

Energy	373kcals/1551kJ
Carbohydrate	8g
of which sugar	4g
Fat	28g
of which saturates	15g
Salt	1g
Fibre	1.5g

Mild creamy chicken curry

Introducing children to more adventurous tastes can be hard,
so start them off with this gently spiced curry.

INGREDIENTS

2 tbsp sunflower oil

1 onion, finely chopped

2 garlic cloves, finely chopped

2–3 tbsp medium curry powder

1 tsp ground cumin

4 skinless boneless chicken
breasts, sliced lengthways
into 4–5 strips

450ml (15fl oz) chicken stock

150g (5¹⁄₂oz) red lentils

150g (5¹⁄₂oz) plain yogurt

salt and freshly ground
black pepper

50g (1³⁄₄oz) toasted flaked almonds

2 tbsp chopped coriander leaves

basmati rice or naan breads,
to serve

SERVES 4   **PREP** 15 MINS   **COOK** 35-40 MINS

1 Heat half the oil in a large, non-stick frying pan that has a lid, and fry the onion for 5 minutes, or until softened, but not browned. Add the garlic and spices and cook for 2 minutes.

2 Add the remaining oil and the chicken and cook for 5–7 minutes, turning to coat the chicken in the spices and to seal it on all sides. Add the stock and lentils and bring to the boil. Cover, reduce the heat, and simmer for 20 minutes, or until the chicken and lentils are cooked.

3 Stir in the yogurt, season to taste, and heat through for 2 minutes until piping hot once more. Do not return to the boil after adding the yogurt, or there is a risk that the curry sauce might split.

4 Sprinkle the curry with the almonds and coriander and serve with basmati rice or warmed naan breads.

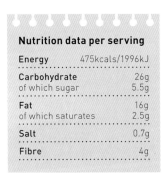

Nutrition data per serving	
Energy	475kcals/1996kJ
Carbohydrate	26g
of which sugar	5.5g
Fat	16g
of which saturates	2.5g
Salt	0.7g
Fibre	4g

Chicken and parsley pot pies

These pies are great to make after a roast chicken dinner or to use up leftover ham, and can also be prepared ahead and stored in the fridge overnight before glazing and baking.

INGREDIENTS

150g (5¹/₂oz) frozen broad beans, or 400g can sweetcorn, drained

50g (1³/₄oz) butter

1 onion, finely chopped

salt and freshly ground black pepper

50g (1³/₄oz) plain flour, plus extra for dusting

450ml (15fl oz) milk

1 tsp Dijon mustard

300g (10oz) cooked chicken, cut into chunky bite-sized pieces

150g (5¹/₂oz) cooked ham, cubed

3 tbsp finely chopped curly or flat-leaf parsley

1 tbsp finely chopped marjoram leaves (optional)

300g (10oz) ready-made rough puff pastry or shortcrust pastry

1 egg, beaten

boiled potatoes and carrots, to serve

SERVES 4    **PREP 20 MINS, PLUS CHILLING**   **COOK 25-30 MINS**

1 Preheat the oven to 200°C (400°F/Gas 6). Place the broad beans or sweetcorn in a bowl and pour over boiling water. Leave for 5–8 minutes, drain, and set aside.

2 Melt the butter in a large pan over a low heat, add the onion, season, and cook for 5–7 minutes until soft and transparent. Remove from the heat and stir in the flour. Pour in a little milk, stir, put back on a low heat, and gradually add the rest of the milk, stirring as you go. You may need to switch to a balloon whisk for a lump-free sauce. Bring to the boil, then reduce to a simmer. Cook for 2–3 minutes, remove from the heat, and stir in the mustard, chicken, ham, herbs, and broad beans. Season and set aside.

3 Roll out the pastry on a lightly floured surface. Cut out 4 small lids, or 1 large lid 4cm (1½in) larger than the basins. Set aside. Spoon the filling into the basins and wet the edges. Drape the lids and press to secure. Make a hole in the top of each pie. Brush with half the beaten egg and chill for 20 minutes, then brush with the remaining egg and bake for 25–30 minutes until golden; cooking a large pie may take a little longer. Remove and serve with boiled potatoes and carrots.

Nutrition data per serving

Energy	703kcals/2942kJ
Carbohydrate	46g
of which sugar	9g
Fat	39g
of which saturates	19g
Salt	2.3g
Fibre	4g

Chinese chicken and rice

Long, slow cooking brings out the delicious, warming flavours of this clay-pot style of Chinese dish, leaving the chicken soft and moreish. Brown rice and seeds add a lovely nutty texture.

INGREDIENTS

1 tsp sesame oil

2 tbsp Chinese rice wine or dry sherry

1 tbsp soy sauce

450g (1lb) skinless boneless chicken thighs, cut into 3cm (1¼in) chunks

2 tbsp sunflower oil

1 red onion, finely chopped

2 garlic cloves, finely chopped

5cm (2in) piece of fresh root ginger, finely chopped

1 green chilli, deseeded and finely chopped

1 tsp five-spice powder

1 litre (1¾ pints) chicken stock

300g (10oz) brown basmati rice

200g (7oz) small broccoli florets

200g (7oz) frozen edamame (soya beans)

2 tbsp pumpkin seeds

2 tbsp sunflower seeds

SERVES 4   **PREP** 10 MINS   **COOK** 1 HR 10 MINS

1 Place the sesame oil, rice wine or sherry, and the soy sauce in a large bowl and mix together well. Marinate the chicken in the mixture for at least 1 hour.

2 Heat the sunflower oil in a lidded, heavy-based saucepan. Drain the chicken from its marinade and fry for 2–3 minutes, until coloured all over. Add the onion, garlic, ginger, and chilli and cook for 2 more minutes. Add the five-spice powder and cook for 1 more minute.

3 Pour the stock and any remaining marinade into the pan, then stir in the rice. Bring to the boil, then reduce to a low simmer, and cook, covered, for 50 minutes, stirring occasionally.

4 Meanwhile, blanch the broccoli and edamame in boiling water for 1 minute, then drain. Dry-fry the pumpkin and sunflower seeds in a non-stick frying pan for 2–3 minutes, until they start to colour and make a popping sound.

5 Stir the blanched vegetables into the rice and cook for a further 5–10 minutes, until the rice is cooked and all the liquid has evaporated. Remove from the heat and leave it to rest, covered, for 5 minutes before mixing in the toasted seeds to serve.

Nutrition data per serving	
Energy	649 kcals/2717kJ
Carbohydrate	69g
of which sugar	3.5g
Fat	22g
of which saturates	3g
Salt	1g
Fibre	7g

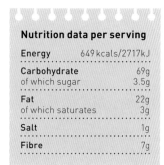

Chicken, onion, and peas

A simple, satisfying dish made with few ingredients.

INGREDIENTS

4 chicken thighs or breasts

salt and freshly ground
    black pepper

2 tbsp oil

1 onion, finely chopped

2 garlic cloves

1 tbsp fresh thyme leaves

600ml (1 pint) mushroom stock
    or vegetable stock

225g (8oz) frozen garden peas

1 tbsp flat-leaf parsley,
    finely chopped

200g (7oz) brown rice

SERVES 4  **PREP** 5 MINS **COOK** 40 MINS

1 Season the chicken well with salt and black pepper. Pour 1 tablespoon of oil into a large, heavy pan and when hot, add the chicken pieces. Cook for about 5 minutes, or until golden, then turn and cook them on the other side for the same length of time. Remove with tongs and set aside.

2 Heat the remaining oil in the pan, add the onion, and cook until soft. Season well, then throw in the garlic and thyme and cook for a few seconds. Return the chicken to the pan and add a small amount of stock. Let it bubble, then stir up any bits from the bottom of the pan before adding the remaining stock. Reduce to a simmer.

3 Tip in the peas and continue to cook, covered, over a low heat for 25–35 minutes, or until the chicken is cooked (the juices should run clear when the chicken is pierced with a sharp knife). If the chicken begins to dry out, top up the pan with a little more hot stock or water.

4 Meanwhile, cook the rice according to the packet instructions. Drain, then serve with the chicken.

Cook's tip: Chicken breasts will not take as long to cook as thighs. To prevent the chicken from drying out, don't have the heat too high.

Nutrition data per serving

Energy	468kcals/1956kJ
Carbohydrate	50g
of which sugar	3.5g
Fat	10.5g
of which saturates	2.2g
Salt	0.8g
Fibre	4.1g

Spicy turkey burgers with avocado cream

These Mexican-inspired burgers are a low-fat alternative to the usual beef burgers. The avocado cream makes a tasty replacement for commercially made ketchup or mayonnaise.

INGREDIENTS

For the patties

450g (1lb) minced turkey

50g (1³⁄₄oz) fresh white breadcrumbs

1 mild red chilli, deseeded and finely chopped

2 heaped tbsp finely chopped coriander

2 large spring onions, trimmed and finely chopped

zest of 1 lime

2 tbsp sunflower oil

For the avocado cream

1 very ripe avocado

1 tsp lime juice

2 heaped tbsp low-fat sour cream

salt and freshly ground black pepper

To serve

4 burger buns

lettuce leaves, sliced tomatoes, cucumber (optional)

SERVES 4   **PREP** 15 MINS   **COOK** 12-15 MINS

1 Place all the ingredients for the patties, except the oil, in a large bowl and mix well. Make sure the mixture is thoroughly combined.

2 Form 4 equal-sized balls of burger mixture. Place them on a chopping board and pat them down on top, and around the edges, to make 4 evenly sized patties. Do not compress the mixture too much, or the burgers will be tough when cooked.

3 Heat the oil in a large frying pan over a medium heat. Fry the patties for 5–6 minutes on each side, or until they are well browned and cooked through.

4 For the avocado cream, mash the avocado and the lime juice together until smooth. Mix in the sour cream and season well.

5 Assemble the burgers by placing the cooked patties in the buns, along with as many fillings as you like, and add a spoonful of avocado cream on top.

Nutrition data per serving

Energy	480 kcals/2009 kJ
Carbohydrate	43g
of which sugar	3g
Fat	18g
of which saturates	4g
Salt	1.4g
Fibre	3.5g

Minted lamb burgers

A real favourite, these burgers are exceptionally tasty and always juicy, as minced lamb has extra fat.

INGREDIENTS

400g (14oz) minced lamb

50g (1¾oz) fresh white breadcrumbs

1 egg yolk

½ red onion, very finely chopped

1 tbsp dried mint, or 2 tbsp finely chopped mint leaves

½ tsp ground cinnamon

½ tsp ground cumin

salt and freshly ground black pepper

To serve

4 burger buns, or 2 large pitta breads, halved

lettuce

tomato

finely sliced red onions

tzatziki

mustard

relish

SERVES 4

 PREP 10 MINS, PLUS CHILLING

 **COOK 10 MINS**

1 Prepare a barbecue for cooking. In a large bowl, mix together all the ingredients for the burgers until well combined.

2 With damp hands (to help stop the mixture sticking to your fingers), divide the mixture into 4 balls and roll each one between your palms until smooth. Flatten each ball out to a large, fat disk, 2.5cm (1in) high, and pat the edges in to tidy them up.

3 Place the burgers on a plate, cover with cling film, and chill for 30 minutes (this helps them keep their shape on cooking).

4 Cook over a hot barbecue for 6–8 minutes, turning as needed, until the meat is springy to the touch and the edges charred.

5 Serve with a selection of buns, or pitta breads, and the suggested accompaniments, and let everyone assemble their own burgers with their preferred fillings.

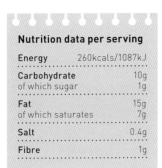

Nutrition data per serving	
Energy	260kcals/1087kJ
Carbohydrate	10g
of which sugar	1g
Fat	15g
of which saturates	7g
Salt	0.4g
Fibre	1g

Sweet and sour chicken

A more sophisticated version of the takeaway
classic – this one has no pineapple chunks.

INGREDIENTS

For the marinade
1 tsp cornflour
1 tbsp soy sauce
1 tbsp rice wine or dry sherry
1 tsp caster sugar

For the chicken
500g (1lb 2oz) skinless boneless
  chicken breast, cut into
  1cm (½in) slices
2 tbsp sunflower oil
2 garlic cloves, finely chopped
2.5cm (1in) fresh root ginger,
  finely chopped
100g (3½oz) raw, unsalted cashew
  nuts, roughly chopped

For the sauce
2 tbsp rice wine vinegar or
  white wine vinegar
2 tbsp rice wine or dry sherry
3 tbsp tomato ketchup
2 tbsp soy sauce
100ml (3½fl oz) chicken stock
1 tbsp caster sugar

SERVES 4  **PREP** 15 MINS, PLUS MARINATING  **COOK** 10 MINS

1 Mix the marinade ingredients in a bowl and turn through the chicken. Cover and refrigerate for at least 30 minutes.

2 Whisk together all the sauce ingredients and set aside.

3 Heat the oil in a wok, add the garlic and ginger, and stir-fry for 1 minute. Add the chicken and stir-fry until it turns pale.

4 Add the sauce and bubble up. Add the nuts and cook for 2–3 minutes until the mixture has thickened and the chicken is coated in a glossy sauce. Serve.

Nutrition data per serving

Energy	386kcals/1616kJ
Carbohydrate	14g
of which sugar	10g
Fat	19g
of which saturates	3.5g
Salt	2.7g
Fibre	1g

Spicy lamb and feta meatballs

These are good with rice or couscous, or even wrapped
up with salad in a tortilla for a quick lunch.

INGREDIENTS

400g (14oz) minced lamb

50g (1³⁄₄oz) fresh white
    breadcrumbs

1 egg, beaten

1 tsp ground cumin

1 tsp paprika

handful of mint leaves, finely
    chopped

salt and freshly ground black
    pepper

60g (2oz) crumbled feta cheese

2 tbsp sunflower oil

couscous, to serve

SERVES 4    **PREP** 10 MINS,
PLUS CHILLING    **COOK** 10 MINS

1 Mix together the minced lamb, breadcrumbs, egg, spices, and mint, and season well. Gently mix in the feta cheese. Cover and chill for about 30 minutes.

2 With damp hands, gently shape walnut-sized balls with the lamb mixture.

3 Heat the oil in a large frying pan and fry the meatballs over a medium heat for 5–7 minutes, until browned all over and cooked through. Serve with couscous.

Nutrition data per serving

Energy	350kcals/1455kJ
Carbohydrate	9g
of which sugar	0.5g
Fat	24g
of which saturates	9g
Salt	1g
Fibre	0.5g

Braised lamb shanks

This takes only minutes to prepare; hours of unattended slow cooking leave it succulent and falling off the bone.

INGREDIENTS

2 tbsp olive oil

4 lamb shanks

salt and freshly ground
   black pepper

3 celery sticks, roughly chopped

3 carrots, roughly chopped

4 shallots, roughly chopped

2 garlic cloves, finely sliced

2 sprigs of rosemary

1 bay leaf

300ml (10fl oz) red wine

450ml (15fl oz) lamb stock

mashed potato, to serve

SERVES 4    **PREP** 15 MINS   **COOK** 3 HRS 15 MINS

1 Preheat the oven to 150°C (300°F/Gas 2). Heat the oil in a very large (4-litre/7-pint) heavy-based flameproof casserole over a medium heat.

2 Add 2 of the shanks to the casserole, season well, and brown for 5 minutes, turning occasionally. Transfer to a plate and set aside. Repeat for the remaining shanks.

3 Add the vegetables and garlic to the casserole and cook over a medium heat for 5 minutes. Return the lamb and its juices and add the herbs, wine, and stock. Bring to the boil and cover. Cook in the oven for 2½–3 hours, or until the meat is starting to fall off the bone.

4 Using a slotted spoon, carefully transfer the shanks and vegetables to a warmed serving dish. Remove the bay leaf and rosemary. Discard the fat from the sauce and pour it into a jug. Serve the lamb and vegetables with mashed potato and the sauce.

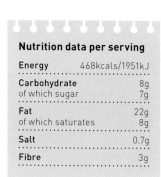

Nutrition data per serving

Energy	468kcals/1951kJ
Carbohydrate	8g
of which sugar	7g
Fat	22g
of which saturates	8g
Salt	0.7g
Fibre	3g

Pearl barley, spinach, and lamb pot

One-pot cooking at its best, this dish is easy to make and full of flavour and goodness.

INGREDIENTS

1 tbsp olive oil

1 onion, finely chopped

2 cloves of garlic, finely chopped

3 carrots, diced

3 celery stalks, diced

few stalks of thyme

750g (1lb 10oz) neck of lamb
on the bone, trimmed of fat

1.2 litres (2 pints) of vegetable stock

75g (2¹/₂oz) pearl barley,
soaked overnight

250g (9oz) spinach leaves,
roughly chopped

salt and freshly ground
black pepper

SERVES 4    **PREP** 15 MINS, PLUS SOAKING   **COOK** 1 HR 25 MINS

1 Heat the oil in a large heavy-based pan, add the onion, and cook over a low heat until it softens. Add the garlic, carrots, celery, and thyme and cook for a further 10 minutes. Add the lamb to the pan and cover with the stock. Bring to the boil and skim off any scum that comes to the surface. Reduce to a simmer, add the pearl barley, and cook gently for 1 hour until the lamb is tender and pearl barley is cooked. Top up with more stock or water if needed.

2 Remove the lamb from the pan, leave to cool slightly, and then shred the meat away from the bone. Meanwhile add the spinach to the pan and cook for 5 minutes, or until it has wilted. Return the lamb to the pot and stir well, then taste and season as required. Ladle into bowls and serve.

Cook's tip: This will taste even better the next day; put in the refrigerator once cooled and reheat when required.

Nutrition data per serving

Energy	570kcals/2731kJ
Carbohydrate	28g
of which sugar	9.5g
Fat	21g
of which saturates	8g
Salt	0.8g
Fibre	5g

Lamb and lentil shepherd's pie with a sweet potato crust

Lentils are an easy way to bulk up a favourite meat dish,
lowering the fat content and boosting the protein. Here they take
on some of the colour and texture of the meat sauce.

INGREDIENTS

100g (3½oz) Puy lentils
2 tbsp olive oil
1 onion, finely chopped
1 celery stick, finely chopped
2 carrots, finely chopped
1 small leek, trimmed and
   finely chopped
1 garlic clove, crushed
450g (1lb) minced lamb
1 tbsp plain flour
500ml (16fl oz) chicken,
   beef, or lamb stock
1 tbsp Worcestershire sauce
1 bay leaf
1 tbsp finely chopped rosemary
salt and freshly ground
   black pepper
700g (1½lb) sweet potatoes,
   peeled and cut into chunks
50g (1¾oz) grated
   Parmesan cheese

SERVES 4    **PREP** 30 MINS   **COOK** 1 HR 30 MINS

1 Place the lentils in a small, heavy-based saucepan. Cover them with cold water, to a depth of at least 3cm (1¼in), and bring to the boil. Cook on a low boil for 5 minutes. Drain and rinse the lentils, and set aside.

2 Heat the oil in a large casserole or heavy-based saucepan. Cook the onion, celery, carrots, and leek for 5 minutes over a medium heat, until they are softened, but not browned. Add the garlic and cook for another minute.

3 Turn the heat up to high and add the lamb to the vegetables. Use a wooden spoon to break up the meat and move it around the pan frequently, until well browned. Stir in the flour, and cook for 1 minute. Add the stock, lentils, Worcestershire sauce, and herbs to the pan, and season to taste. Bring to the boil, and then reduce to a low simmer. Cook the lamb, uncovered, for 50 minutes to 1 hour until the sauce has reduced almost completely and the lentils are soft. If the stock evaporates before the end of the cooking time, add a little water.

4 Meanwhile, boil the sweet potatoes for 10–15 minutes, until tender, and drain them well. Transfer to a pan, add the Parmesan, and mash well. Season to taste, cover, and keep warm.

5 Preheat the oven to 200°C (400°F/Gas 6). Remove the rosemary and bay leaf from the lamb and place the lamb in a 20cm (8in) square ovenproof dish. Top with the mashed sweet potato and bake for 30 minutes until the top is golden brown.

Nutrition data per serving

Energy	620kcals/2596kJ
Carbohydrate	56g
of which sugar	15g
Fat	26g
of which saturates	10.5g
Salt	1.2g
Fibre	11g

Pork stir-fry with cashew nuts and greens

A fast and flavoursome dish.

INGREDIENTS

2 tbsp sunflower oil

1 onion, chopped

2.5cm (1in) piece of fresh root ginger, peeled and finely chopped

3 garlic cloves, finely chopped

1 red chilli, deseeded and finely sliced

400g (14oz) pork tenderloin, finely sliced

3 tbsp soy sauce

1 tbsp sesame oil

handful of cashew nuts

200g (7oz) bok choy, roughly sliced lengthways

SERVES 4  **PREP** 15 MINS   **COOK** 10-15 MINS

1 Heat the oil in a wok, add the onion and stir-fry quickly for a minute then add the ginger, garlic, and chilli and cook, stirring continually to make sure the ingredients don't burn.

2 Throw in the pork, stir, and cook for 3–5 minutes until no longer pink, then add the remaining ingredients and cook for a further 3–5 minutes, stirring occasionally until the bok choy is tender and wilted. Serve immediately with noodles or rice.

Nutrition data per serving

Energy	265kcals/1100kJ
Carbohydrate	6g
of which sugar	4g
Fat	16g
of which saturates	3g
Salt	2.3g
Fibre	2g

Lebanese spiced beef and okra

A spiced and flavourful one-pot dish.

INGREDIENTS

1 tbsp olive oil

1 onion, sliced

200g (7oz) okra, topped and halved horizontally

500g (1lb 2oz) lean steak, cut into 1cm (½in) pieces

1 tsp paprika

4 cloves garlic, finely chopped

juice of ½ lemon

400g can of chopped tomatoes

handful of fresh coriander, roughly chopped

salt and freshly ground black pepper

brown rice, to serve (optional)

SERVES 4   **PREP** 10 MINS   **COOK** 35 MINS

1 Heat the oil in a large frying pan, add the onion, and cook over a medium heat for 2 minutes until it begins to soften, then add the okra and cook for a further minute.

2 Add the beef, paprika, and garlic and cook, stirring, until the beef is no longer pink. Add the lemon juice, tomatoes, and coriander and season with salt and pepper. Bring to the boil then reduce to a simmer and cook, uncovered, for 20–30 minutes, stirring occasionally, until the sauce has reduced and thickened. Spoon into warmed bowls and serve. You could accompany this with some brown rice.

Cook's tip: Frying the okra before the other ingredients are added will prevent it from becoming gluey.

Nutrition data per serving

Energy	226kcals/947kJ
Carbohydrate	7.5g
of which sugar	6g
Fat	8.5g
of which saturates	2.5g
Salt	0.4g
Fibre	3g

Beef and bean stew

A hearty meal-in-one of tender beef simmered
with tomatoes and beans.

INGREDIENTS

2 tbsp olive oil

2 onions, roughly chopped

salt and freshly ground black
pepper

500g (1lb 2oz) lean beef, diced

1 tsp hot paprika or cayenne pepper

1 tbsp cider vinegar

4 garlic cloves, finely chopped

400g can of black-eyed beans,
drained and rinsed

400g can of chickpeas, drained
and rinsed

400g can of chopped tomatoes

300ml (10fl oz) vegetable stock
handful of fresh flat-leaf
parsley, chopped

4 spring onions, finely chopped,
to serve

SERVES 4    **PREP** 10 MINS   **COOK** 35 MINS

1 Heat the oil in a large pan, add the onions, and cook for about
5 minutes until soft. Season with salt and black pepper, then add
the beef and paprika or cayenne pepper, stir to coat, and cook for
2–3 minutes until the beef is no longer pink. Add the vinegar and
cook for a minute or two until the liquid evaporates.

2 Add the garlic and cook for 1 minute, then tip in the beans and
chickpeas and stir to combine. Add the tomatoes and stock, bring
to the boil, then reduce to a simmer and cook gently for 20–30 minutes
until thickened. Top up with a little extra stock or water if it dries out
too much. Stir in the parsley and adjust the seasoning if required.
Scatter over the chopped spring onions and serve straight away.

Nutrition data per serving

Energy	453kcals/1910kJ
Carbohydrate	40g
of which sugar	8g
Fat	14g
of which saturates	3g
Salt	0.6g
Fibre	8g

Pasta primavera

This delicate, tasty sauce is an easy and delicious way to get
plenty of green vegetables into your family's diet.

INGREDIENTS

salt and freshly ground
    black pepper
100g (3½oz) sugarsnap peas
125g (4½oz) fine asparagus
    spears, halved
100g (3½oz) baby courgettes,
    quartered lengthways
400g (14oz) dried linguine
    or fettuccine
1 tbsp olive oil
2 garlic cloves, finely sliced
1 shallot, finely chopped
2 tbsp extra virgin olive oil
150ml (5fl oz) half-fat crème
    fraîche
½ tsp grated nutmeg
finely grated zest of 1 lemon,
    plus juice of ½ lemon
2 tbsp torn basil leaves
2 tbsp chopped flat-leaf
    parsley leaves
100g (3½oz) baby spinach
Parmesan cheese shavings
    and ciabatta, to serve

SERVES 4   **PREP** 10 MINS   **COOK** 20 MINS

1 Bring a large pan of salted water to the boil and add the sugarsnap
peas, asparagus, and courgettes. Return to the boil and cook for
3 minutes, or until the vegetables are just tender, but still brightly
coloured and al dente. Drain well, then run under cold water to set
the colour. Drain once more, and set the vegetables aside in the
colander over the kitchen sink.

2 Refill the pan used for cooking the vegetables with more salted
water and bring it to the boil. Cook the pasta according to the
packet instructions. Meanwhile, heat the olive oil in a small pan
over a medium heat and sauté the garlic and shallot for 2 minutes.

3 In a medium jug, combine the extra virgin olive oil, crème fraîche,
nutmeg, lemon zest and juice, basil, and parsley. Add the cooked
garlic and shallot. Stir well and season generously with pepper.

4 Drain the pasta well in the same colander as the vegetables, to
reheat them slightly, then return the pasta and vegetables to the
pan. Add the spinach and stir until it wilts. Add the herby sauce to
the pasta and stir to coat.

5 Transfer to warmed serving bowls, top with Parmesan shavings,
and serve with ciabatta.

Nutrition data per serving

Energy	505kcals/2135kJ
Carbohydrate	73g
of which sugar	4.5g
Fat	15g
of which saturates	5g
Salt	0.1g
Fibre	6.5g

Spaghetti Bolognese

A household standard, but the long, slow cooking time
here turns the everyday into something special.

INGREDIENTS

SERVES 4   PREP 20 MINS   COOK 1 HR

2 tbsp olive oil

1 onion, finely chopped

1 celery stick, finely chopped

1 carrot, finely chopped

2 garlic cloves, crushed

500g (1lb 2oz) minced beef

400g can chopped tomatoes

250ml (9fl oz) beef stock

1 tbsp tomato purée

1 tsp caster sugar

2 tbsp roughly chopped flat-leaf
   parsley leaves

1 tsp dried oregano

salt and freshly ground
   black pepper

300g (10oz) dried spaghetti

finely grated Parmesan cheese,
   to serve

1 Heat the oil in a large, heavy-based saucepan and cook the onion, celery, and carrot over a medium heat for 5 minutes, until softened, but not browned. Add the garlic and cook for 1 minute. Add the minced beef and cook it over a high heat, breaking any clumps up with a wooden spoon and turning to brown all over.

2 Add the tomatoes and stock. Stir in the tomato purée, sugar, parsley, and oregano, and season generously. Slowly bring to the boil, then reduce the heat to a low simmer, and cook for 1 hour, or more if needed, until the sauce has thickened and reduced, and smells rich.

3 When the sauce is nearly ready, cook the spaghetti until just al dente in boiling salted water according to the packet instructions. Drain the pasta (reserving about a ladleful of the cooking water) and return it to the pan along with the reserved water.

4 Toss the sauce through the spaghetti so that it coats the pasta, and serve with plenty of Parmesan.

Nutrition data per serving

Energy	641kcals/2692kJ
Carbohydrate	60g
of which sugar	10g
Fat	27g
of which saturates	10g
Salt	0.6g
Fibre	6g

Classic carbonara

Even when you think you have nothing in the fridge, you
may have the ingredients for this creamy sauce.

INGREDIENTS

200g (7oz) streaky bacon rashers

salt and freshly ground
    black pepper

400g (14oz) dried long pasta, such
    as spaghetti, linguine, fettuccine,
    or pappardelle

200ml (7fl oz) single cream

4 eggs, lightly beaten

40g (1¼oz) finely grated Parmesan
    cheese, plus extra to serve

2 tbsp chopped flat-leaf parsley
    leaves, to garnish

tomato and basil salad, to serve

SERVES 4    **PREP** 15 MINS    **COOK** 25 MINS

1 Heat a large, non-stick frying pan over a medium heat. Add the bacon and cook, turning, until crisp. Transfer the bacon to a plate lined with kitchen paper.

2 Bring a large pan of salted water to the boil and cook the pasta according to the packet instructions.

3 Meanwhile, measure the cream into a jug and stir in the eggs, Parmesan, and season with pepper. Snip the bacon into pieces with kitchen scissors, and stir into the egg.

4 Drain the pasta and return to the pan, pour in the egg mixture, and place over a low heat. Stir for 2 minutes, or until the sauce has thickened and clings to the strands of pasta. Divide between warmed bowls, season with a little more pepper, and sprinkle with parsley. Serve with extra Parmesan and a tomato and basil salad.

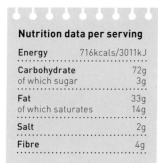

Nutrition data per serving

Energy	716kcals/3011kJ
Carbohydrate	72g
of which sugar	3g
Fat	33g
of which saturates	14g
Salt	2g
Fibre	4g

Crispy gnocchi with Bolognese sauce

If you have some Bolognese sauce in the freezer, this tasty, family-friendly meal can be ready in minutes.

INGREDIENTS

1 tbsp olive oil
1 onion, finely chopped
2 garlic cloves, finely chopped
500g (1lb 2oz) lean minced beef
1 tsp dried oregano
1 tsp dried marjoram
500g carton passata
150ml (5fl oz) red wine
1 bay leaf
salt and freshly ground black pepper
500g (1lb 2oz) shop-bought gnocchi
50g (1³/₄oz) fresh white breadcrumbs
40g (1¹/₄oz) finely grated Parmesan cheese
rocket salad, to serve

SERVES 4    **PREP** 20 MINS    **COOK** 1 HR 30 MINS

1 Heat the oil in a large pan over a medium heat and fry the onion for 5 minutes. Add the garlic and cook for 2 minutes.

2 Stir the meat into the pan and cook for 5 minutes, breaking it up with a wooden spoon, or until browned. Stir in the dried herbs, passata, wine, and bay leaf. Season well and bring to the boil, then reduce the heat, partially cover, and simmer gently for 1 hour, stirring occasionally. Preheat the oven to 190°C (375°F/Gas 5).

3 Put the gnocchi in a shallow ovenproof dish. Mix the breadcrumbs, Parmesan, and plenty of pepper in a bowl.

4 Pour the Bolognese sauce over the gnocchi and sprinkle with the cheesy breadcrumbs. Place the dish on a baking tray and bake for 15 minutes, or until the crumbs are crispy. Spoon onto plates and serve with rocket salad.

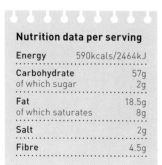

Nutrition data per serving

Energy	590kcals/2464kJ
Carbohydrate	57g
of which sugar	2g
Fat	18.5g
of which saturates	8g
Salt	2g
Fibre	4.5g

Ricotta and squash ravioli

Make the ravioli a day in advance. Dust them with polenta, place them on a tray covered with cling film, and chill.

INGREDIENTS

175g (6oz) butternut squash, peeled, deseeded, and cut into 5cm (2in) cubes
1 tbsp olive oil
salt and freshly ground black pepper
85g (3oz) ricotta cheese
30g (1oz) Parmesan cheese, finely grated
1 garlic clove, crushed
$\frac{1}{2}$ tsp freshly grated nutmeg
350g (12oz) pasta dough
plain flour, for dusting
polenta or fine cornmeal, for dusting

For the sage butter

3 tbsp olive oil
60g (2oz) butter
zest of $\frac{1}{2}$ lemon
2 tsp roughly chopped sage leaves
finely grated Parmesan cheese, to serve

SERVES 4   **PREP** 30 MINS, PLUS CHILLING   **COOK** 50-55 MINS

1 For the filling, preheat the oven to 200°C (400°F/Gas 6). Place the butternut cubes in a roasting tin and drizzle over the oil, 3 tablespoons water, and seasoning. Cover with foil and roast for 30–35 minutes, or until tender. Transfer to a food processor and blitz until smooth. Spread in the roasting tin and leave until cold. Place the ricotta, Parmesan, garlic, and nutmeg in a bowl. Stir in the butternut squash and season to taste. Chill.

2 Roll out the pasta dough onto a lightly floured surface to 3mm ($\frac{1}{8}$in) thick. Cut out 64 rounds using a cutter. Top half the rounds with $\frac{1}{2}$ teaspoon filling. Brush a little water around the filling and place a plain pasta round on top. Pinch the edges to seal. This will make 32 ravioli. Dust with polenta or cornmeal to prevent them from sticking together. Cover and chill until required.

3 Bring a large pan of salted water to the boil. Add the pasta and cook for 4–5 minutes or until al dente. For the sage butter, heat a large frying pan, add the olive oil, butter, lemon zest, and sage, and sauté for 30 seconds. Remove and add plenty of pepper. Drain the pasta in a colander, add to the frying pan, and toss well to mix. Serve sprinkled with Parmesan.

Nutrition data per serving	
Energy	640kcals/2670kJ
Carbohydrate	53g
of which sugar	3g
Fat	40g
of which saturates	15g
Salt	1.2g
Fibre	3g

Roasted vegetable lasagne

Meat-free days are a good thing, but sometimes difficult to manage
for the whole family. This makes them easy.

INGREDIENTS

3 tbsp olive oil

2 red onions, roughly chopped

1 aubergine, cut into
   2.5cm (1in) cubes

1 red pepper, cut into
   2.5cm (1in) pieces

1 yellow pepper, cut into
   2.5cm (1in) pieces

1 courgette, cut into 2.5cm
   (1in) cubes

1 bulb fennel, finely sliced

3 garlic cloves, roughly chopped

1 tsp dried rosemary

1 tsp dried basil

salt and freshly ground
   black pepper

500ml (16fl oz) tomato passata

400ml (14fl oz) half-fat crème
   fraîche

2 eggs, beaten

60g (2oz) finely grated
   Parmesan cheese

225g (8oz) fresh lasagne sheets

100g (3½oz) grated
   mozzarella cheese

garlic bread, to serve

SERVES 4    **PREP** 25 MINS   **COOK** 1 HR 5 MINS

1 Preheat the oven to 200°C (400°F/Gas 6). Pour the oil into a large roasting tin and heat in the oven for 5 minutes.

2 Add all the vegetables to the tin with the garlic, herbs, and plenty of seasoning. Stir well and return the tin to the oven for 30 minutes, stirring occasionally. Remove, then stir the passata into the roasted vegetables.

3 Meanwhile, place the crème fraîche, eggs, and Parmesan in a jug, season with pepper, and whisk together with a fork. Place half the vegetables in the base of a 28 x 20 x 5cm (11 x 8 x 2in) ovenproof dish and top with half the lasagne. Repeat the layers.

4 Pour the egg mixture over the lasagne and top with the mozzarella. Place the dish on a baking tray and bake for 30 minutes. Serve with hot garlic bread.

Nutrition data per serving

Energy	635kcals/2660kJ
Carbohydrate	46g
of which sugar	9g
Fat	36g
of which saturates	17g
Salt	0.7g
Fibre	6g

Butternut squash risotto

It's well worth roasting the squash before adding it to the risotto;
it gives a lovely deep, rich, sweet flavour.

INGREDIENTS

1 butternut squash, approx.
    800g (1¾lb) prepared weight

2 tbsp olive oil, plus extra
    for drizzling

1 onion, finely chopped

1 garlic clove, finely chopped

700ml (1 pint 3½fl oz) hot vegetable
    stock or chicken stock

300g (10oz) risotto rice, such as
    Arborio or Carnaroli

small glass of white wine (optional)

2 tbsp chopped sage leaves

60g (2oz) finely grated Parmesan
    cheese, plus extra to serve

1 tbsp butter (optional)

salt and freshly ground
    black pepper

SERVES 4-6   **PREP** 10 MINS   **COOK** 1 HR 25 MINS

1 Preheat the oven to 200°C (400°F/Gas 6). Slice the squash in half lengthways and scoop out the seeds. Place on a baking tray, drizzle with oil, and cover with foil. Bake for 1 hour, until soft.

2 When the squash is nearly cooked, start the risotto. Heat the oil in a large, heavy-based, deep-sided frying pan. Cook the onion over a medium heat for 5 minutes. Add the garlic and cook for a further minute.

3 Keep the stock simmering on the stove near the risotto pan. Add the rice to the onion pan, and stir. When it sizzles, pour in the wine (if using) and allow to evaporate. Add stock a ladleful at a time, stirring, for 20 minutes, allowing the liquid to evaporate between ladlefuls.

4 Scoop out the squash flesh and mash it, or purée in a food processor, with 2 tablespoons of stock.

5 Add the squash and sage to the risotto and cook for 5 minutes, until most of the liquid has evaporated. The rice should be cooked, but still al dente. Add the Parmesan and butter (if using), and season. Serve with extra Parmesan.

Nutrition data per serving

Energy	553kcals/2316kJ
Carbohydrate	73g
of which sugar	10g
Fat	14g
of which saturates	6g
Salt	0.8g
Fibre	5g

Aubergine stuffed with goat's cheese, pine nuts, and apricots

Take inspiration from the Middle East to transform aubergines into a delicious vegetarian main course.

INGREDIENTS

2 large aubergines

2 tbsp olive oil, plus extra for rubbing

30g (1oz) pine nuts

1 red onion, finely sliced

1 garlic clove, crushed

50g (1¾oz) dried apricots, finely chopped

75g (2½oz) fresh white breadcrumbs

100g (3½oz) firm goat's cheese, finely chopped, or crumbled

2 tbsp finely chopped dill fronds

2 tbsp finely chopped mint leaves

1 tsp smoked paprika

salt and freshly ground black pepper

SERVES 2-4  **PREP 20 MINS** **COOK 50 MINS**

1 Preheat the oven to 190°C (375°F/Gas 5). Halve the aubergines lengthways and cut a criss-cross into the cut side, without piercing the skin. Rub with oil and bake, cut-sides up, for 30 minutes. Scoop out the interior, leaving a shell of 5mm (¼in). Chop the flesh.

2 Heat a large frying pan and dry-fry the pine nuts for 3–4 minutes. Put them in a bowl and wipe the pan with kitchen paper.

3 Heat the oil in the pan. Cook the onion for 5 minutes, until soft. Add the aubergine flesh. Cook for 3–4 minutes, then add the garlic for 1 minute.

4 Add the onion mixture to the pine nuts with the apricots, breadcrumbs, goat's cheese, herbs, and smoked paprika, and season.

5 Divide the stuffing between the aubergine halves and bake for 20 minutes, until golden brown.

Nutrition data per serving	
Energy	328kcals/1369kJ
Carbohydrate	24g
of which sugar	10.5g
Fat	21g
of which saturates	6g
Salt	0.8g
Fibre	6g

Pumpkin and coconut curry

The sweet flesh of pumpkin complements creamy coconut milk perfectly. Add chopped red chilli for more heat.

INGREDIENTS

1 tbsp vegetable oil

1 red onion, finely chopped

2 garlic cloves, finely chopped

700g (1½lb) pumpkin or butternut squash flesh, cut into 2.5cm (1in) cubes

4 tbsp medium curry paste

250ml (9fl oz) vegetable stock

300ml (10fl oz) reduced-fat coconut milk

salt and freshly ground black pepper

rice, to serve

SERVES 4  **PREP 15 MINS**  **COOK 30 MINS**

1 Heat the vegetable oil in a large saucepan placed over a medium heat. Add the onion and fry for 5 minutes until it has softened, but not browned. Add the garlic and cook for a further 2 minutes, until it smells fragrant, but has not burned or turned dark brown.

2 Increase the heat to high, add the pumpkin or butternut squash cubes, and cook for 2 minutes, stirring constantly so that mix does not catch on the base of the pan.

3 Reduce the heat to medium and stir in the curry paste to coat, then cook for 2 minutes, stirring occasionally.

4 Add the stock and coconut milk, season, and stir well to combine. Increase the heat and bring the curry to the boil, then reduce the heat to a gentle simmer.

5 Cover and simmer very gently for 20 minutes, or until the flavours and textures are harmonious. Stop the cooking when the pumpkin is tender, but not falling apart. Serve with rice.

Nutrition data per serving

Energy	212kcals/890kJ
Carbohydrate	18g
of which sugar	10g
Fat	13.5g
of which saturates	7g
Salt	0.6g
Fibre	4g

SWEETS AND SNACKS

Baked Parmesan and rosemary crisps

These easy home-baked crisps transform
a simple wrap into a gourmet snack.

INGREDIENTS

4 large wraps

2 tbsp olive oil

2 tsp rosemary leaves,
finely chopped

4 tbsp finely grated
Parmesan cheese

freshly ground black pepper

hummus or baba ghanoush,
to serve

SERVES 4    **PREP** 5 MINS   **COOK** 5-7 MINS

1 Preheat the oven to 200°C (400°F/Gas 6). Lay the wraps on a
work surface and brush all over on both sides with the olive oil.

2 Scatter them with the rosemary and Parmesan and season well
with pepper. Place on a baking tray.

3 Bake them at the top of the oven for 5–7 minutes until golden
brown, puffed up, and crispy. Watch them carefully for the last
minute, as they burn quickly.

4 Remove them from the oven, then transfer to a wire rack to cool.
When they are cool, break them into jagged, irregular pieces and
serve with hummus or baba ghanoush.

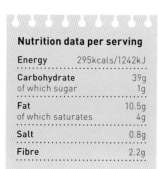

Nutrition data per serving

Energy	295kcals/1242kJ
Carbohydrate	39g
of which sugar	1g
Fat	10.5g
of which saturates	4g
Salt	0.8g
Fibre	2.2g

Barbecued corn on the cob with lime and chilli butter

This butter is an easy way to flavour grilled meat, fish, or vegetables. It freezes well for up to six months.

INGREDIENTS

100g (3½oz) unsalted
    butter, softened
finely grated zest of 1 lime
½ tsp chilli powder or
    cayenne pepper
½ tsp sea salt
freshly ground black pepper
4 sweetcorn cobs
a little olive oil

SERVES 4   **PREP** 10 MINS
PLUS CHILLING   **COOK** 10 MINS

1 Heat a barbecue. In a small bowl, mash the butter with the lime zest, chilli powder or cayenne pepper, sea salt, and black pepper.

2 Cut a square of greaseproof paper, about 15cm (6in) square. Put the butter in the middle of one edge of the paper and shape it like a sausage. Roll the butter sausage up in the paper, then twist the ends like a Christmas cracker so the butter forms a tight shape. Leave in the freezer for at least 30 minutes before use (or freeze until needed).

3 Cook the sweetcorn cobs in a large pan of boiling water for up to 5 minutes until the corn is tender (this will depend on the size and age of the cobs). Drain well, rub them in a little oil, and grill for 6 minutes over a hot barbecue, turning them frequently, until they are lightly charred on all sides.

4 Serve the sweetcorn with a 1cm- (½in-) thick disk of the chilled butter on top to melt.

Nutrition data per serving	
Energy	287kcals/1195kJ
Carbohydrate	16g
of which sugar	2g
Fat	23g
of which saturates	13g
Salt	0.6g
Fibre	2g

Breadsticks with pepper dip

These party nibbles come in three different flavours,
but if preferred, simply dust with polenta.

INGREDIENTS

350g (12oz) white bread flour,
  plus extra for dusting
2 tsp fast-action dried yeast
2 tsp caster sugar
1 tsp salt
2 eggs
2 tbsp olive oil
vegetable oil, for brushing
4 tbsp poppy seeds
4 tbsp sesame seeds
6 tbsp finely grated
  Parmesan cheese

For the roasted pepper dip
2 large red peppers
4 garlic cloves, unpeeled
3 tbsp olive oil
1 tsp smoked paprika
1/2 tsp caster sugar
1/2 tsp ground cumin
1/2 tsp salt
dash of Tabasco sauce

MAKES 18    **PREP 15 MINS, PLUS RISING**   **COOK 45-50 MINS**

1 Preheat the oven to 220°C (425°F/Gas 7). Sift the flour, yeast, sugar, and salt into a large bowl. Lightly beat 1 egg with the olive oil and 250ml (9fl oz) lukewarm water, add to the dry ingredients, and mix to form a dough. Transfer to a lightly floured surface and knead for 5 minutes. Return to the bowl, cover with oiled cling film, and leave to rise in a warm place for about 1 hour until doubled in size.

2 Meanwhile, roast the peppers on a baking tray for 15–20 minutes until lightly charred. Add the garlic and cook for a further 10 minutes. Transfer the peppers and garlic to a plastic bag and leave to cool. Core and deseed the peppers and peel off the skin. Pop the garlic from their skins. Combine with the remaining ingredients in a food processor and blitz to a coarse dip.

3 Lightly oil 2 baking sheets. Roll out the dough to a fat sausage and cut into 18 equal-sized pieces. Roll each piece into a stick 12cm (5in) long. Scatter the seeds and Parmesan onto 3 separate plates. Beat the remaining egg. Brush the sticks with the beaten egg and roll a third of the sticks in each flavour. Place them a little apart on the baking sheets and bake for 15–20 minutes, or until crisp and golden. Allow to cool.

Nutrition data per serving

Energy	158kcals/662kJ
Carbohydrate	16g
of which sugar	2.5g
Fat	9.5g
of which saturates	2.5g
Salt	0.4g
Fibre	1.5g

Sesame rice crackers

These fiery hot crackers are perfect for serving with
dips or spicy relishes and pickles.

INGREDIENTS

500g (1lb 2oz) sticky rice
(sushi rice), washed in cold
running water, until the
water runs clear

salt

2 tbsp sesame seeds

1 tsp wasabi paste

2 tsp tamari (soy sauce)

sunflower oil, for frying

hot carrot and onion seed
pickle or spicy cauliflower
pickle, to serve

SERVES 6    **PREP** 20 MINS, PLUS DRYING    **COOK** 20 MINS

1 Tip the washed rice into a large pan, add 600ml (1 pint) cold water, cover with a lid, bring to the boil, and simmer for 10 minutes, or until all the water has been absorbed; make sure it doesn't dry out or the rice will burn. Remove from the heat, but do not remove the lid. Leave covered for 15 minutes.

2 Season the cooked rice with salt, stir in the sesame seeds, wasabi, and tamari, and mix well until it is all combined.

3 Spread the mixture out onto a baking tray lined with baking parchment. Squash the rice a little and top with another sheet of baking parchment. Use a rolling pin to roll over the paper and flatten the rice so it is about 5mm (¼in) thick. Remove the baking parchment and place in the fridge to dry overnight.

4 Remove the rice from the fridge 20 minutes before you are ready to cook. Pour the oil to a depth of 5cm (2in) in a deep frying pan. Slice the rice into square shapes, breaking pieces off (it will be irregular), and add to the hot oil a couple at a time. Continue frying until they are all cooked. Drain on kitchen paper and serve with a hot carrot and onion seed or spicy cauliflower pickle.

Nutrition data per serving

Energy	363kcals/1514kJ
Carbohydrate	62g
of which sugar	1g
Fat	7g
of which saturates	1g
Salt	0.6g
Fibre	0.5g

Lavosh with aubergine dip

Iranian-style seeded crisp breads served with a sesame-scented aubergine dip make a great snack or appetizer.

INGREDIENTS

150g (5¹/₂oz) plain flour, plus extra for dusting

¹/₂ tsp salt

2 egg whites

15g (¹/₂oz) butter, melted

2 tbsp sesame seeds

1 tbsp poppy seeds

For the dip

2 medium aubergines

2 garlic cloves, crushed

zest and juice of 1 lemon

3 tbsp tahini paste

¹/₂ tsp salt

90ml (3fl oz) olive oil

3 tbsp finely chopped fresh coriander

4 tbsp Greek yogurt

freshly ground black pepper

SERVES 8   **PREP** 20 MINS, PLUS COOLING    **COOK** 1 HR 10 MINS

1 Preheat the oven to 200°C (400°F/Gas 6). For the dip, bake the aubergines on a baking tray for 30–40 minutes, or until soft and lightly charred. Leave to cool.

2 Meanwhile, make the lavosh. Sift the flour and salt into a large bowl. Beat 1 egg white with 90ml (3fl oz) water, stir into the flour with the melted butter, and mix well to form a dough. Lightly knead the dough on a floured surface, divide into 6 balls, and roll out each ball until paper thin, then place on baking sheets. Repeat with all the dough.

3 Brush the remaining egg white over the lavosh, sprinkle the seeds, and bake in 2 batches for 10–15 minutes, or until crisp and golden.

4 Halve the aubergines and scoop the flesh into a food processor. Add the rest of the ingredients and blend to a chunky spread. Check the seasoning, spoon into a bowl, and serve with the crisp breads.

Cook's tip: You can also store the lavosh, after it has cooled, in an airtight container for 2–3 days. Re-crisp in a warm oven. The dip can be stored for 2–3 days in an airtight container in the fridge.

Nutrition data per serving

Energy	226kcals/994kJ
Carbohydrate	15.5g
of which sugar	1.5g
Fat	17g
of which saturates	3.5g
Salt	0.6g
Fibre	3g

Mini naan toasts with roasted vegetables and goat's cheese

These pretty little appetizers taste as delicious as they look, and can be prepared well in advance.

INGREDIENTS

$^1/_2$ aubergine, approx. 150g (5$^1/_2$oz), cut into 1cm ($^1/_2$in) cubes

$^1/_2$ red pepper, approx. 100g (3$^1/_2$oz), cut into 1cm ($^1/_2$in) cubes

1 courgette, approx. 125g (4$^1/_4$oz), cut into 1cm ($^1/_2$in) cubes

$^1/_2$ red onion, approx. 100g (3$^1/_2$oz), finely chopped

2 tbsp olive oil, plus extra if needed

salt and freshly ground black pepper

2 plain naan breads

100g (3$^1/_2$oz) soft goat's cheese

100g (3$^1/_2$oz) cream cheese

2 tbsp finely chopped basil leaves

MAKES 40    **PREP** 30 MINS, PLUS COOLING   **COOK** 35 MINS

1 Preheat the oven to 200°C (400°F/Gas 6). Put the aubergine, red pepper, courgette, and onion in a large roasting tin in a single layer. Toss with the olive oil and season.

2 Cook for 20 minutes, turning after 15 minutes, until soft and charred at the edges. Set aside to cool, adding $^1/_2$ tablespoon of oil if they look dry. Check the seasoning.

3 Meanwhile, cut the naan breads into small circles using a 4cm (1$^1/_2$in) round cutter and put on a baking tray. Cook for 10–15 minutes until golden brown and crispy. Set aside to cool.

4 In a bowl, beat the goat's cheese, cream cheese, and basil, and season well. When ready to serve, spread each piece of bread with a little herby goat's cheese and top with 1 teaspoon of vegetables, pressing down slightly so the vegetables stick to the cheese.

Nutrition data per serving

Energy	45kcals/189kJ
Carbohydrate	3.5g
of which sugar	0.5g
Fat	3g
of which saturates	1g
Salt	0.15g
Fibre	0.5g

Oven-baked potato skins with soured cream dip

These crispy potato skins are a real hit at a party and are a reasonably healthy option, as well as fun to eat.

INGREDIENTS

4 large baking potatoes

2 tbsp sunflower oil

salt and freshly ground
   black pepper

150ml (5fl oz) soured cream

4 spring onions, finely sliced

SERVES 4    **PREP** 10 MINS   **COOK** 20 MINS

1 Preheat the oven to 200°C (400°F/Gas 6). Bake the potatoes in the oven for up to 1 hour, until they are cooked through. Set aside to cool; this will make cutting them more manageable.

2 Cut each potato in half and scoop out all but 5mm (¼in) of the potato from the skins. Set this aside for another time, perhaps to make mashed potato or fishcakes. Cut each halved potato skin into 4 long, thin slices. Brush on all sides with oil and place, skin-side down, on a baking tray. Sprinkle them with salt and return to the oven for 20 minutes, until crispy and golden brown on top.

3 Mix together the soured cream and spring onions, and season well. Serve the potato skins with the soured cream dip.

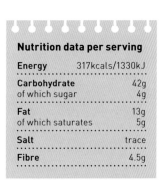

Nutrition data per serving	
Energy	317kcals/1330kJ
Carbohydrate	42g
of which sugar	4g
Fat	13g
of which saturates	5g
Salt	trace
Fibre	4.5g

Tuna and sweetcorn melts

A few hot snacks are welcome at a children's party,
and these melts are always popular.

INGREDIENTS

8 x 1cm- (½in-) thick slices
 of baguette

2 tbsp olive oil

185g can of tuna, drained

50g (1¾oz) canned sweetcorn,
 drained

2 spring onions, finely chopped
 (optional)

2 tbsp mayonnaise

75g (2½oz) grated cheese,
 such as Cheddar

salt and freshly ground
 black pepper

MAKES 8    **PREP** 5 MINS    **COOK** 10-15 MINS

1 Preheat the oven to 220°C (425°F/Gas 7). Place the slices of baguette on a baking sheet and brush both sides with a little oil. Bake at the top of the oven for 5–7 minutes, turning once, until lightly browned on both sides. Set aside.

2 In a bowl, mash together the tuna, sweetcorn, spring onions (if using), mayonnaise, and half the cheese, and season well.

3 Divide the topping equally between the baguette slices, and top each piece with some of the remaining cheese. Bake the slices in the hot oven for a further 5–7 minutes, until they are hot and the cheese has melted to a nice golden brown. Remove from the oven and allow to cool for at least 5 minutes before serving.

Nutrition data per serving

Energy	243kcals/1022kJ
Carbohydrate	23g
of which sugar	2g
Fat	11.5g
of which saturates	3.5g
Salt	1g
Fibre	1.5g

Tuna empanadas

Originally from Spain and Portugal, these savoury pastries called empanadas translate as "wrapped in bread".

INGREDIENTS

450g (1lb) plain flour, plus extra for dusting

sea salt

85g (3oz) unsalted butter, cut in cubes

2 eggs, lightly beaten, plus extra for glazing

For the filling

1 tbsp olive oil, plus extra for greasing

1 onion, finely chopped

120g canned tomatoes, drained weight

2 tsp tomato purée

140g can of tuna, drained

2 tbsp finely chopped parsley

freshly ground black pepper

MAKES 24    **PREP** 45 MINS   **COOK** 40-50 MINS

1 To make the pastry, sift the flour into a bowl with ½ teaspoon salt. Add the butter and rub it in. Mix in the eggs with 4–6 tablespoon of water. Wrap in cling film and chill for 30 minutes.

2 Heat the oil in a frying pan, add the onion, and fry over a medium heat for 5 minutes. Add the tomatoes, tomato purée, tuna, and parsley, and season with pepper. Reduce the heat and simmer for 10–12 minutes, stirring occasionally. Allow to cool.

3 Preheat the oven to 190°C (375°F/Gas 5). Roll out the pastry to 3mm (⅛in) thick. Cut out 24 rounds with a 9cm (3½in) round cutter. Put 1 teaspoon of the filling on each. Brush the edges with water, fold over, and pinch together.

4 Place on an oiled baking tray and brush with egg. Bake for 25–30 minutes. Serve warm.

Nutrition data per serving

Energy	115kcals/484kJ
Carbohydrate	14g
of which sugar	0.7g
Fat	4.5g
of which saturates	2g
Salt	0.15g
Fibre	1g

Crispy king prawns with teriyaki sauce

Use good-quality, juicy prawns for this simple dish
as they are the star of the show.

INGREDIENTS

3 tbsp tamari (soy sauce)

1 tbsp mirin

1 tsp caster sugar

2–3 tbsp cornflour

salt and freshly ground
   black pepper

pinch of dried chilli flakes

12 large raw king prawns, shelled
   and deveined, but tail left intact

5 tbsp sunflower oil

SERVES 4    **PREP 15 MINS**   **COOK 10 MINS**

1 First make the teriyaki sauce by mixing together the tamari, mirin, and caster sugar. Taste, adjust if necessary, and set aside.

2 Mix together the cornflour, salt and pepper, and chilli flakes, then add the prawns and toss well so they all get thoroughly coated.

3 Heat the oil in a wok or pan until hot, add a few prawns, and cook until they turn pink, about 3–5 minutes. Remove with a slotted spoon and continue until all the prawns are cooked. Serve with the teriyaki sauce, either spooned over the prawns or as a dip.

Cook's tip: You could also use rice flour or potato flour to coat the prawns.

Nutrition data per serving

Energy	234kcals/971kJ
Carbohydrate	8g
of which sugar	2g
Fat	17g
of which saturates	2g
Salt	2.4g
Fibre	trace

Sesame prawn toast

Ready in minutes and great to serve as a canapé with drinks.
If you omit the chilli from the prawn mixture, they make a
delicious home-from-school snack for children.

INGREDIENTS

250g (9oz) ready-cooked prawns

1 red chilli, deseeded and
   finely chopped

handful of fresh coriander leaves,
   finely chopped

salt and freshly ground black
   pepper

8 slices of white bread, lightly
   toasted

4 tbsp sesame seeds, or more
   if needed

4–5 tbsp sunflower oil, or more
   if needed

MAKES 32    **PREP** 15 MINS    **COOK** 15-20 MINS

1 Place the prawns in a food processor along with the chilli, coriander, and salt and pepper and whizz until really well minced. Slice the crusts off the bread and reserve (see Cook's tip).

2 Spread the minced prawn mixture over the toast slices and press down well to make sure it sticks. Cut the toasts into quarters and then triangles. Tip the sesame seeds out onto a plate and dip each toast, prawn-side down, into them to cover.

3 Heat 1 tablespoon oil in a frying pan over a medium heat. Add a few toasts at a time, plain-side down, and cook for 1–2 minutes, then turn and cook the topped side for 1–2 minutes, or until golden. Remove and place on kitchen paper. Remove excess sesame seeds from the pan and continue until all the toasts are done, topping up with the remaining oil as needed.

Cook's tip: Use the bread crusts to make breadcrumbs: whizz in a food processor and keep sealed in the fridge for a few days, or in the freezer for up to 3 months.

Nutrition data per serving

Energy	43kcals/182kJ
Carbohydrate	3g
of which sugar	0.2g
Fat	3g
of which saturates	0.5g
Salt	0.2g
Fibre	0.3g

Olive pinwheels

Light puff pastry spread with tapenade, rolled and
baked until golden makes for a delectable party snack.

INGREDIENTS

400g (14oz) ready-made
    rough puff pastry
1 egg, lightly beaten, to glaze

For the tapenade
150g (5¹/₂oz) pitted black olives
2 garlic cloves, roughly chopped
salt and freshly ground black
    pepper
100ml (3¹/₂fl oz) extra virgin olive oil
juice of ¹/₂ lemon

MAKES 16    **PREP** 20 MINS   **COOK** 15-20 MINS

1 Preheat the oven to 200°C (400°F/Gas 6). For the tapenade, whizz the olives, garlic, and seasoning in a food processor until well minced. With the blade turning, trickle in enough oil to make a soft paste; you may not need it all. Add a little lemon juice to taste, then set aside.

2 Roll the pastry out to a rectangle about 30 x 35cm (12 x 14in); this may be more easily done between sheets of cling film. Spread the tapenade over the pastry leaving a 2.5cm (1in) border all around the edge of the pastry.

3 Carefully roll up the pastry from the shorter end, as tightly as you can, then cut into 16 slices. Sit the pinwheels on their sides on a lightly oiled baking sheet and brush each one with a little egg. Bake in the oven for 15 minutes, or until pale golden and lightly puffed. Remove and transfer to a serving plate. Serve as a snack with drinks.

Cook's tip: Make these ahead and freeze them raw, then simply bake in the oven from frozen. You can replace the tapenade with a pesto, a tomato sauce, or simply grated cheese.

Nutrition data per serving

Energy	154kcals/642kJ
Carbohydrate	9g
of which sugar	0.3g
Fat	12.5g
of which saturates	4g
Salt	0.4g
Fibre	0.4g

Three-cheese scones

These tasty scones make a great addition to a picnic, lunch box, or just as a savoury teatime treat.

INGREDIENTS

30g (1oz) butter, cut into cubes, plus extra for greasing

175g (6oz) self-raising flour, sifted, plus extra for dusting

½ tsp mustard powder

salt and freshly ground black pepper

50g (1¾oz) grated Cheddar cheese

25g (scant 1oz) finely grated Parmesan cheese

1 egg, lightly beaten

3–4 tbsp milk, plus extra for brushing

25g (scant 1oz) grated Red Leicester cheese

butter, or cream cheese with garlic and herbs, to serve

SERVES 6  **PREP** 15 MINS  **COOK** 10-15 MINS, PLUS COOLING

1 Preheat the oven to 200°C (400°F/Gas 6). Grease a baking sheet with butter. Place the flour and mustard powder in a medium mixing bowl, and season well. Add the butter to the bowl and rub it in with your fingertips until the mixture resembles breadcrumbs.

2 Stir in the Cheddar and Parmesan cheeses and the egg. Add enough of the milk to form a soft scone dough.

3 Roll out the dough on a well-floured surface to a thickness of about 2cm (¾in). Cut out 6 scones, using a 6cm (2½in) round cutter, re-rolling the dough as necessary.

4 Place the scones on the prepared baking sheet. Brush them with milk and sprinkle over the Red Leicester cheese.

5 Bake for 10–15 minutes. Remove from the oven, transfer to a wire cooling rack, and allow to cool for 10–15 minutes.

6 Split the scones in half and serve warm, spread with butter, or cream cheese with garlic and herbs.

Nutrition data per serving

Energy	257kcals/1076kJ
Carbohydrate	21g
of which sugar	0.8g
Fat	14g
of which saturates	8g
Salt	0.9g
Fibre	1g

Quick cheese pastries

These pastries make appetizing canapés for a party in minutes. Make more than you think you'll need!

INGREDIENTS

215g (7½oz) sheet ready-rolled
  puff pastry, approx. 20 x 25cm
  (8 x 10in)
4 tsp ready-made green pesto
4 tsp tapenade
30g (1oz) grated mozzarella cheese
25g (scant 1oz) goat's cheese
1 egg, lightly beaten

MAKES 8

 **PREP** 15 MINS, PLUS COOLING

 **COOK** 10-15 MINS

1 Preheat the oven to 200°C (400°F/Gas 6). Line 2 baking sheets with baking parchment.

2 Unroll the pastry and divide it into 4 equal strips. Cut each strip into 4 equal pieces to give 16 equal-sized rectangles.

3 Place 8 rectangles on the sheets. Top 4 of them with 1 teaspoon pesto each, and 4 of them with 1 teaspoon tapenade each.

4 Sprinkle the mozzarella over the pesto-topped squares and divide the goat's cheese between the tapenade-topped squares.

5 Brush the edges of the topped squares with beaten egg, and place one of the reserved pastry pieces on top of each one. Carefully, but firmly, press the edges of the pastry together with a fork to seal.

6 Brush each parcel with beaten egg and bake for 10–15 minutes, or until golden. If baking on 2 oven shelves, swap the positions of the baking sheets halfway through the cooking time, to give all the pastries time at the top of the oven. Transfer to a wire rack to cool slightly for 5 minutes, and serve warm.

Nutrition data per serving

Energy	147kcals/615kJ
Carbohydrate	9.5g
of which sugar	0.5g
Fat	10.5g
of which saturates	4.5g
Salt	0.4g
Fibre	0g

Buttermilk scones

Home-made, these are one of the simplest and best teatime
treats. Buttermilk makes the lightest scones.

INGREDIENTS

60g (2oz) unsalted butter,
  chilled, and cut into pieces,
  plus extra for greasing
250g (9oz) strong white bread
  flour, plus extra for dusting
2 tsp baking powder
½ tsp salt
175ml (6fl oz) buttermilk, plus
  extra if needed
reduced-sugar jam,
  to serve

MAKES 6-8  **PREP 15-20 MINS**  **COOK 12-15 MINS**

1 Preheat the oven to 220°C (425°F/Gas 7). Line a baking sheet with
baking parchment and grease it. Sift the flour, baking powder, and
salt into a chilled bowl. Add the butter.

2 Rub with your fingertips until the mixture forms fine crumbs,
working quickly. Make a well in the centre and, in a steady stream,
pour in the buttermilk. Quickly toss with a fork. Do not over-mix.

3 Stir the mixture until the crumbs form a dough. Add a little more
buttermilk if it seems dry. Turn onto a floured surface and knead
for a few seconds; keep it rough, not smooth. Pat the dough out to a
round 2cm (¾in) thick.

4 Cut out with a 7cm (2¾in) round pastry cutter. Pat out the
trimmings and cut additional rounds until all the dough has been
used. Arrange the scones so they are about 5cm (2in) apart on the
prepared baking sheet. Bake in the hot oven for 12–15 minutes until
lightly browned and risen. Serve immediately with reduced-sugar jam.

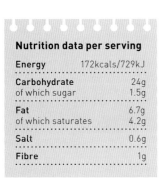

Nutrition data per serving

Energy	172kcals/729kJ
Carbohydrate	24g
of which sugar	1.5g
Fat	6.7g
of which saturates	4.2g
Salt	0.6g
Fibre	1g

French crêpes

Even if you make pancakes only once a year, a good, stress-free
recipe will help you to cook them with style!

INGREDIENTS

100g (3½oz) plain flour
2 eggs, lightly beaten
200ml (7fl oz) whole milk
20g (¾oz) butter, melted
sunflower oil, for cooking
For the filling
sliced fruit
ground cinnamon

MAKES 8    **PREP** 10 MINS,
PLUS RESTING   **COOK** 15-20 MINS

1 Sift the flour into a large jug. Add the eggs and 4 tablespoons of the
milk and, using an electric hand-held whisk, whisk well to combine.

2 Gradually add the remaining milk, whisking constantly. Stir in
both the melted butter and 75ml (2½fl oz) of cold water. Whisk
well to give a thin, smooth batter. Set aside to rest for 30 minutes,
covered with a clean tea towel.

3 Brush the base of an 18cm (7in) non-stick frying pan with a little
oil. Heat over a high temperature on the hob.

4 Carefully pour in just enough batter to coat the base of the
pan and swirl the pan to give an even layer of batter. Cook for
40–60 seconds, or until the pancake is set. Flip over using a palette
knife and cook the other side, reducing the hob temperature if the
pancake is browning too quickly.

5 Remove from the pan and place on a warmed plate. Repeat to
cook 7 more pancakes, occasionally brushing the pan with more oil.
Stack the pancakes up with a sheet of greaseproof paper between each,
and cover the stack with foil to keep them all warm. Serve the pancakes
with bowls containing the fillings.

Nutrition data per serving	
Energy	124kcals/519kJ
Carbohydrate	10g
of which sugar	1.5g
Fat	7g
of which saturates	3g
Salt	0.1g
Fibre	0.5g

Acknowledgments

The Diabetes Cooking Book (2010) **Authors** Fiona Hunter and Heather Whinney; **Art director** Luis Peral; **Food stylist** Cara Hobday; **Prop stylist** Victoria Allen; **Home economists** Richard Harris, Emily Shardlow, and Rachel Wood; **Out-of-house editors** Helena Caldon and Fiona Corbridge; **Project editors** Robert Sharman and Saloni Talwar; **Designers** Katherine Raj and Devika Dwarkadas; **Senior creative art editor** Caroline de Souza.

The Gluten-Free Cookbook (2012) **Authors** Fiona Hunter, Jane Lawrie, and Heather Whinney; **Recipe editors** Jane Bamforth and Holly Kyte; **Recipe testers** Rebecca Blackstone, Anna Burges-Lumsden, Amy Carter, Jan Fullwood, Laura Fyfe, Katy Greenwood, Anne Harnan, Catherine Rose, and Rachel Wood; **Food stylists** Marie-Ange Lapierre and Emily Jonzen; **Hand model** Danaya Bunnag; **Senior editors** Alastair Laing and Chitra Subramanyam; **Project art editors** Katherine Raj, Prashant Kumar, and Anamica Roy.

Family Kitchen Cookbook (2013) **Author** Caroline Bretherton; **Nutritionist** Fiona Hunter; **New photography** Lis Parsons, William Reavell, and Stuart West; **Photography art direction** Susan Downing, Geoff Fennell, Lisa Pettibone, and Penny Stock; **Food styling** Emma-Jane Frost, Paul Jackman, Jane Lawrie, Rosie Reynolds, and Penny Stephens; **Prop styling** Susan Downing, Liz Hippisley, and Wei Tang; **Photography shoot manager** Anne Fisher; **Consultant for Babies and Toddlers chapter** Rosan Meyer; **Recipe testers** Jane Bamforth, Ramona Andrews, Anna Burges-Lumsden, Amy Carter, Sue Davie, Francesca Dennis, Hulya Erdal, Georgina Fuggle, Jan Fullwood, Anne Harnan, Richard Harris, Sue Harris, Jo Kerr, Sarah King, Emma Lahaye, Bren Parkins-Knight, Ann Reynolds, Cathy Seward, Rachel Wood, and Amanda Wright; **Senior editors** Scarlett O'Hara and Dorothy Kikon; **Senior art editors** Sara Robin and Ivy Roy; **Editors** Lucy Bannell.

Family Nutrition (2014) **Author** Jane Clarke; **Recipe consultant** Caroline Bretherton; **Nutritionist** Fiona Hunter; **Recipe tester** Katy Greenwood; **Prop stylist** Isabel de Cordova; **Food stylist** Jane Lawrie; **New photography** William Reavell; **Senior editors** Camilla Hallinan and Ira Sharma; **Project art editor** Katherine Raj and Simran Kaur; **Editors** Carolyn Humphries and Diana Vowles; **Designers** Mandy Earey, Saskia Janssen, and Simon Murrell.